15-25
29-30
33, 89

61-62
35-38
65

WITHDRAWN

550
Ross

Recent Revolutions
in Geology

RECENT REVOLUTIONS IN GEOLOGY

RECENT REVOLUTIONS IN GEOLOGY
Lisa A. Rossbacher

FRANKLIN WATTS 1986
NEW YORK LONDON
TORONTO SYDNEY
A SCIENCE IMPACT BOOK

TMC
550
Ross

Frontispiece: an Apollo 15 view of the Earth

Diagrams by Vantage Art, Inc.

Photographs courtesy of: NASA/Johnson Space Center: pp. 2, 108, 109, 112; U.S. Geological Survey: pp. 39, 43, 55, 59, 63; P.R. Carlson, U.S. Geological Survey: p. 40; National Oceanographic and Atmospheric Administration: pp. 42, 49; R.T. Holcomb, U.S. Geological Survey: p. 56; G.E. Lewis, U.S. Geological Survey: p. 71; NASA: p. 83; NASA/Jet Propulsion Laboratory: pp. 86, 87, 95, 96, 99; E.A. Cernan/NASA: p. 90; EROS Data Center, U.S. Geological Survey: p. 105.

Library of Congress Cataloging-in-Publication Data

Rossbacher, Lisa A.
Recent revolutions in geology.

(A Science impact book)
Bibliography: p.
Includes index.
Summary: Surveys recent theories and discoveries in geology, including research into plate tectonics, theories of mass extinctions, and new perspectives on the earth caused by studying the geology of other planets.
1. Geology—Juvenile literature. [1. Geology]
I. Title. II. Series.

QE29.R76 1986   550   86-9236
ISBN 0-531-10242-4

Copyright © 1986 by Lisa A. Rossbacher
All rights reserved
Printed in the United States of America
6 5 4 3 2 1

CONTENTS

11 ACKNOWLEDGMENTS

13 INTRODUCTION

CHAPTER 1
DRIFTING CONTINENTS:
15 THE PLATE TECTONICS REVOLUTION

CHAPTER 2
27 HOW DO WE KNOW THE CONTINENTS MOVE?

CHAPTER 3
35 EXPLORING THE OCEAN FLOOR

CHAPTER 4
47 RICHES FROM THE SEA

CHAPTER 5
53 PREDICTING VOLCANIC ERUPTIONS

CHAPTER 6
61 UNDERSTANDING EARTHQUAKES

CHAPTER 7
67 WHAT KILLED THE DINOSAURS?

CHAPTER 8
EXPLAINING EXTINCTIONS
75 IN GEOLOGIC HISTORY

CHAPTER 9
EXTRATERRESTRIAL GEOLOGY:
81 THE MOON AND BEYOND

CHAPTER 10
REVOLUTION AT THE
93 EDGE OF THE SOLAR SYSTEM

CHAPTER 11
GEOLOGY MEETS
103 SPACE-AGE TECHNOLOGY

115 GLOSSARY

119 FURTHER READING

121 INDEX

ALSO BY
LISA A. ROSSBACHER

CAREER OPPORTUNITIES
IN GEOLOGY AND
THE EARTH SCIENCES

RECENT REVOLUTIONS IN GEOLOGY

TO DALLAS

ACKNOWLEDGMENTS

A number of people contributed to the information and ideas presented in this book. Some of the information came from the public lectures at the Comparative Planetolgy meeting held at the California Institute of Technology in June 1985. A presentation by Eugene Shoemaker of the U.S. Geological Survey was especially informative. Study of the Earth using technologies from space was a major topic at a NASA-sponsored workshop that was held in January 1985 in Oracle, Arizona. Particular thanks go to the organizers of that meeting—Nick Short, James Head, and Victor Baker—for providing a forum for wide-ranging discussions about new perspectives on Earth and the science of geology in the space age. I have also profited from conversations with Mason Hill, Kathryn Sullivan, John Everett, and Ronald Greeley.

Carole Edwards, photo librarian for the U.S. Geological Survey, was extremely helpful in finding suitable photographs. The National Oceanographic and Atmospheric Administration and the National Aeronautics and Space Administration, through the Johnson Space Center (Houston) and the Jet Propulsion Laboratory (Pasadena), also provided photographs.

A special acknowledgment and a place in heaven belong to the people who have read and commented constructively on various parts of this book. This list notably includes William Wadsworth, Dallas Rhodes, and Horacio Ferriz, all of Whittier College, and Henry Rasof, my editor at Franklin Watts. Most of all, I need to thank my husband and colleague, Dallas Rhodes. His support, insight, and sense of humor contributed more than he can know.

INTRODUCTION

> *Every great scientific truth goes through three stages. First, people say it conflicts with the Bible. Next, they say it has been discovered before. Lastly, they say they always believed it.*
>
> —Louis Agassiz

Science is still happening, changing, and advancing. Textbooks and lectures sometimes present science as a collection of dry facts discovered long ago, to be memorized but not questioned. This is very wrong. The nature of all science is to keep growing; this includes geology, the study of the Earth. In fact, a number of important changes in geology have occurred in recent years. Several of these changes are the subject of this book.

All important discoveries are revolutionary because they change the way we look at the world and our relationship to it. Plate tectonics is one of the new developments in geology that qualifies as a revolution. Other recent revolutions in geology are related to the plate tectonics revolution: new approaches to mineral exploration; a new understanding of the ocean floor; new theories for the major events in Earth history, especially the disappearance of the dinosaurs; and a growing success with predicting earthquakes and volcanic eruptions. Discoveries about the other planets—and about our own planet from space—have given us a new perspective on Earth and its history.

Our current understanding of Earth's geology is not engraved in stone. It, too, will change as new discoveries are made. One day, new theories may replace some of the ideas described in this book. And that's a good sign. When geology stops changing, it stops being a science.

CHAPTER 1
DRIFTING CONTINENTS: THE PLATE TECTONICS REVOLUTION

If the fit between South America and Africa is not genetic, surely it is a device of Satan for our frustration.

—Chester Longwell

A volcano erupts in Colombia. Earthquakes rattle windows in San Francisco and cause thousands of deaths in Mexico City. Mt. Everest rises a few centimeters every year. A new sea floor is being created in the middle of the Atlantic Ocean. Could all these events have anything in common?

Strangely, they do. They are all explained by the theory of **plate tectonics.** This theory provides a way of understanding, in a global sense, the forces that shape the surface of the Earth. The wide acceptance of this theory shows how the concept of plate tectonics represents a major revolution in the science of geology.

The theory of plate tectonics simply states that the Earth's surface is broken into a number of hard plates, like pieces of an eggshell (Figure 1). These plates are not fixed in one place. They move slowly around the planet's surface, pushed and pulled by the flow of hot material deeper in the Earth. This movement of the surface plates is responsible for

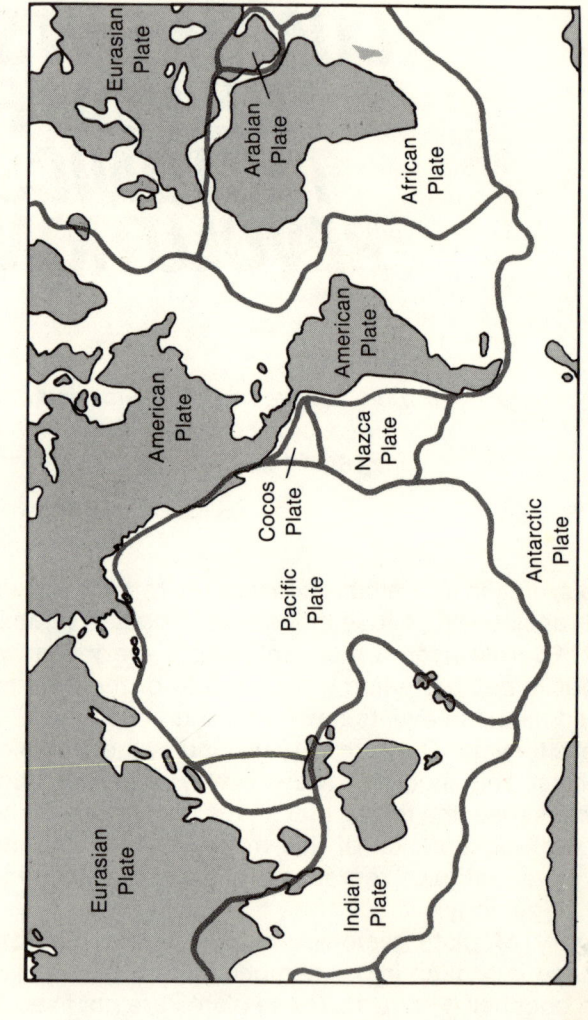

Figure 1. The theory of plate tectonics says that the surface of the Earth is divided into about nine large plates, like a broken eggshell, and a number of smaller ones. The larger plates are shown here.

phenomena such as earthquakes and volcanoes, for the creation of mountains, and for the larger features on the entire planet.

NEW IDEAS FOR AN OLD EARTH

To understand why plate tectonics is considered a revolution in geological thinking, we need to know a little about how the theory developed. Traditional ideas about the Earth were that the continents and oceans were permanent features on the Earth's surface. Not only did this fit the Biblical story of Earth history, but no one could imagine *how* the continents would be able to move across the Earth's surface.

As the first accurate world maps became available, scientists began noticing that the edges of the continents looked like a huge jigsaw puzzle. The English philosopher Francis Bacon commented on this in 1620, and the same observation caused the German scientist Alfred Wegener to make a formal proposal about it in 1912. Wegener called this apparent movement of land masses across the Earth's surface **continental drift** (Figure 2). At the time, few people took Wegener's suggestion very seriously because no one could guess what could make the continents plow across the ocean floor.

Other observations that could not be explained by the "static" theory of Earth history involved the locations of many rocks and fossils. The distributions of these could be explained only if the continents were once all pushed together into one giant landmass. For example, deposits left by glaciers occur in the Saharan Desert, and oil has been discovered in arctic regions. These findings did not fit current conditions in those areas.

Another example is the discovery of fossils from a distinctive plant, *Glossopteris*, that lived during the Permian period of geologic time, from 280 to 225 million years ago. Fossil leaves of this fern-like plant are found in rocks of that age on several continents: Australia, South America, Africa, and Antarctica. If the continents were pushed together, the land areas with these fossil plants would form one large

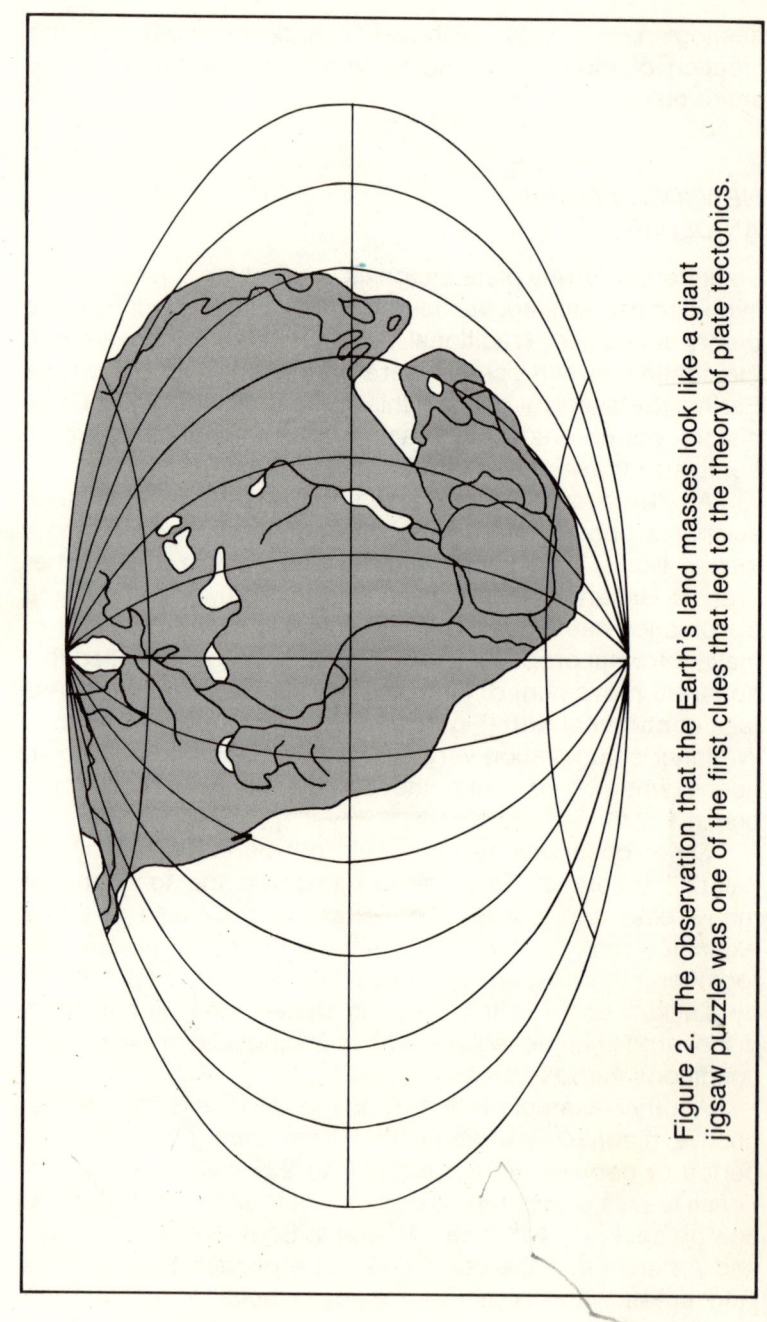

Figure 2. The observation that the Earth's land masses look like a giant jigsaw puzzle was one of the first clues that led to the theory of plate tectonics.

patch, showing where this plant lived during the Permian period.

The answer to the problem of how the continents could have moved came from exploration of the ocean floor. The traditional view of the Earth was that the sea floors had been created at the same time as the Earth, 4.5 billion years ago. When a new round of ocean exploration began in the 1940s, some scientists expected the ocean crust to record the entire history of the planet. Instead, they discovered that even the oldest sea floor was less than 200 million years old. Sea floor so young (compared with the age of the Earth) must still be in the process of being formed.

Additional study of the ocean floor showed that the youngest rocks in the ocean are along the mid-ocean ridges on the sea floor. These huge underwater mountain ranges extend for thousands of miles, but only in a few cases, like in Iceland, do their crests rise above sea level. The farther the rocks are from the mid-ocean ridges, the older they are.

The traditional idea that the ocean floors were formed at the same time as the Earth cannot explain these observations. The theory of plate tectonics can.

THE PLATES

The hard, rigid plates that form the outermost portion of the Earth are about 60 miles (100 kilometers, or km) thick. These plates include both the Earth's crust and the upper mantle (Figure 3).

The rocks of the crust are composed mostly of minerals with light elements, like aluminum and sodium, while the mantle contains some heavier elements, like iron and magnesium. Together, the crust and upper mantle that form the surface plates are called the **lithosphere.** This rigid layer floats on the denser material of the lower mantle the way a wooden raft floats on a pond. The plates are supported by a weak, plastic layer of the lower mantle called the **asthenosphere.** Also like a raft on a pond, the lithospheric plates are carried along by slow currents in this more fluid layer beneath them.

With an understanding of plate tectonics, geologists have put together a new history for the Earth's surface.

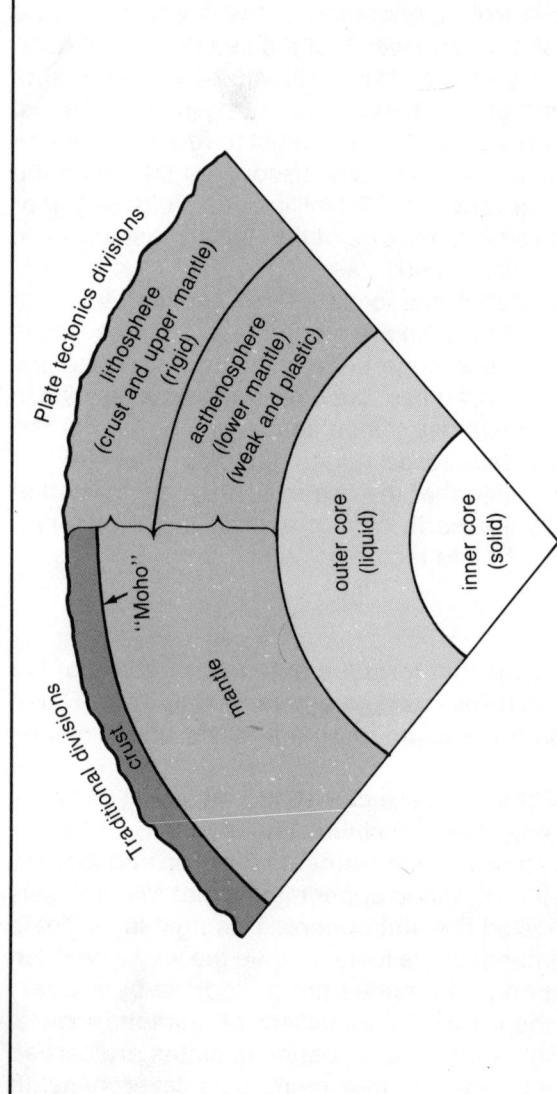

Figure 3. The layers of the Earth's interior, according to the theory of plate tectonics. The traditional divisions of crust, mantle, and core are grouped differently; the crust and upper mantle together form the hard lithosphere, and the soft lower mantle material is called the asthenosphere.

About 200 million years ago, the plates at the Earth's surface formed a "supercontinent" named *Pangaea* (pan-GEE-ah) by Wegener. ("Pangaea" combines the Greek words for "all" and "Earth.") When this supercontinent started to tear apart because of plate movement, Pangaea first broke into two large continental masses with a newly formed sea that grew between the land areas as the depression filled with water. The southern one—which included the modern continents of South America, Africa, Australia, and Antarctica—is called *Gondwanaland*. The northern one—with North America, Europe, and Asia—is called *Laurasia*. North America tore away from Europe about 180 million years ago, forming the northern Atlantic Ocean.

Some of the lithospheric plates have ocean floor on them, and others carry land masses or a combination of the two types. As the plates slowly move around at the Earth's surface, they are like bumper cars in slow motion—running into each other, pulling apart, or grinding past one another. The edges of the plates, where these collisions and separations happen, is where many earthquakes and volcanoes occur.

THE EDGE OF THE PLATES

The movement of the lithospheric plates is responsible for earthquakes, volcanoes, and Earth's largest mountain ranges. Our current understanding of the interaction between different plates explains why these occur where they do. For example, the edge of the Pacific Ocean has been called "The Ring of Fire" because so many volcanic eruptions and earthquakes happen there. Before the 1960s, geologists could not explain why active volcanoes and strong earthquakes were concentrated in that region. The theory of plate tectonics gave them an answer.

Earthquakes happen as the plates grind past each other, sticking for a while and then jerking ahead. Volcanoes result from heat deep beneath the Earth's surface, which melts rock material to form lava. Mountains can be pushed up as two plates run into each other.

When two plates carrying land masses collide, the plates are pushed together. What happens can be seen by pushing together two books lying on a table against each other. The pressure will force the edges of the two books to bulge upward. When two plates carrying continents run into each other, the crust folds and thickens, and mountains are formed. The Alps and the Himalayan Mountains were created in this way.

When one of the plates involved in a collision has ocean floor at its leading edge, it will dive out of the way as the other plate moves over it (Figure 4). Something similar happens when two pieces of paper lying on a table are pushed together. One will go over the other. As long as one of the lithospheric plates has ocean floor, it doesn't matter whether the other is carrying a continent or more ocean floor. When this happens to plates at the Earth's surface, the process is called **subduction** (sub-DUCK-shun).

This sliding of one plate over another is not a smooth, continuous movement. Sharp jerks occur as one plate grinds its way over the lower one, and these sudden movements create earthquakes. These quakes originate down to about 430 miles (700 km) beneath the Earth's surface. Below this depth, the rocks are probably too hot to be rigid, and they just ooze past one another.

A plate with ocean crust that is forced down under the upper plate heats up. Eventually the rocks that form the plate will melt and become **magma,** the hot, molten rock beneath the Earth's surface. Magma may work its way up toward the surface, where it flows out as lava and builds volcanoes. Thus, earthquakes and volcanoes are both associated with collisions between lithospheric plates. Japan is a good example of an area with geologic activity associated with a subduction zone today.

A fracture where two bodies of rock are moving past each other is a **fault**. Some of the most famous faults in the world occur where two plates are sliding past each other. The San Andreas Fault in California is a well-known example of this. It traces the break between the Pacific Plate, which is moving north relative to the North American Plate (Figure 5). Friction between the two plates causes pressure to build up;

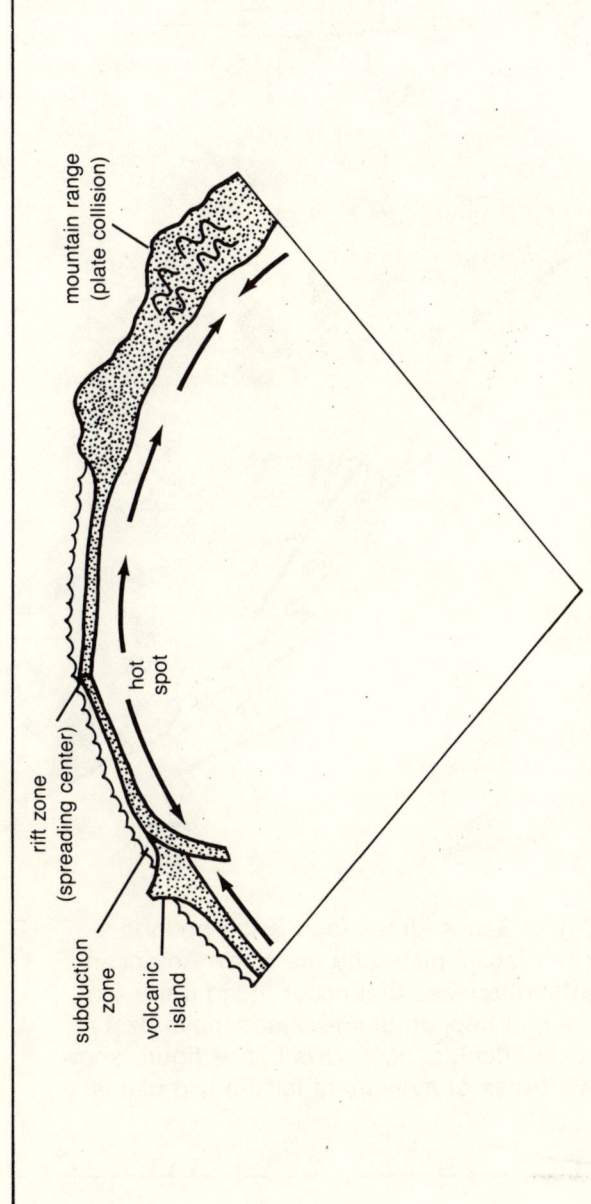

Figure 4. Several types of activity at the edges of plates are shown in this cross section. Crustal material, forming the top layer of the plates, is shown with a dotted pattern. Continental crust is thicker than oceanic crust, but both are exaggerated here.

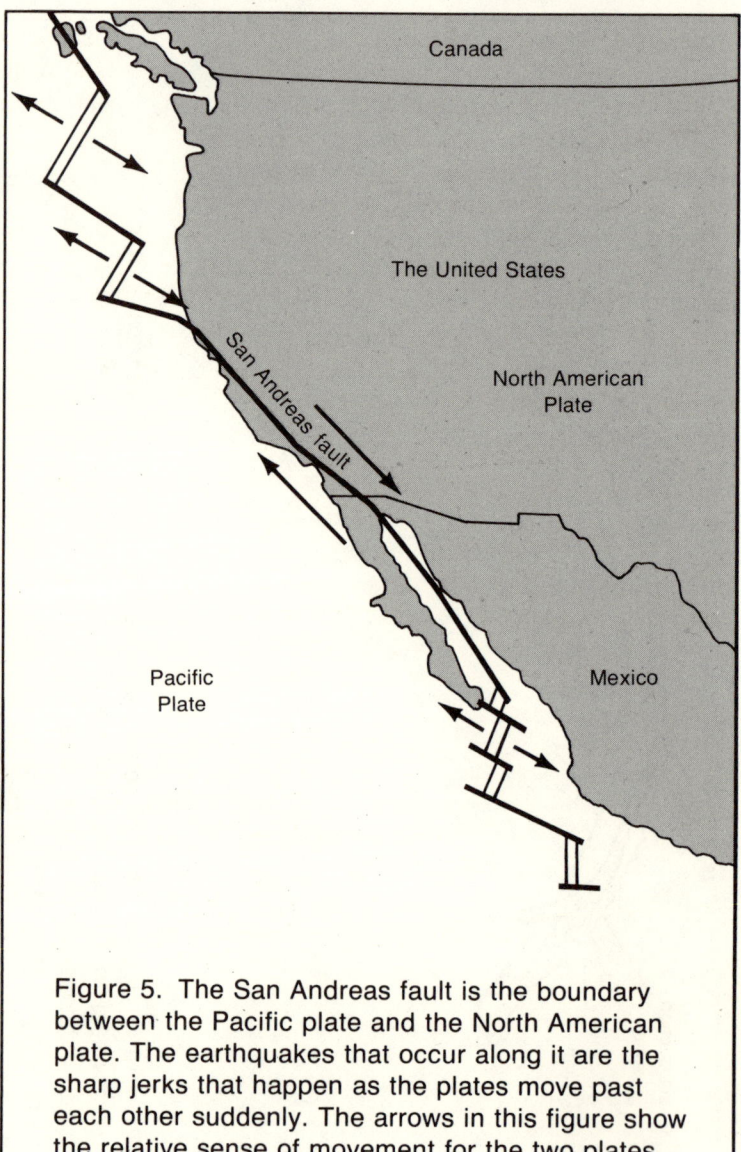

Figure 5. The San Andreas fault is the boundary between the Pacific plate and the North American plate. The earthquakes that occur along it are the sharp jerks that happen as the plates move past each other suddenly. The arrows in this figure show the relative sense of movement for the two plates.

this stress is finally released in sudden earthquakes. Some parts of the San Andreas have frequent small quakes, while other areas build up stress for a long time, resulting in major earthquakes that sometimes have catastrophic consequences.

Plate movement along the San Andreas will eventually have other effects, too. In 15 million years, Los Angeles and San Francisco will be next-door neighbors. Continued plate movement around the world may one day in the distant future result in another supercontinent.

FORMATION OF NEW CRUST

As collisions destroy lithospheric plates at their edges, new crust is created where the plates pull apart. Places where new material is forming are called **rift zones** or **spreading centers.** As plates pull away from each other, hot magma rises into the break between the plates. This magma cools into rock and is slowly carried away as the plates continue to pull apart. More magma then flows toward the rift from below, and the process continues. This process of plate tectonics, often called **sea-floor spreading,** helps explain sea-floor studies showing that the youngest rocks are found along the mid-ocean ridges—the spreading centers. Iceland is a good example of a spreading center exposed above sea level.

The three major ocean basins of Earth—the Pacific, Atlantic, and Indian oceans—were created as the sea floor spread, opening up between the surrounding land masses. The sea floors tell many stories about continental drift. This information is collected by ocean exploration, by deep-sea drilling, and by using tiny submarines called **submersibles.**

In 1957, Bruce Heezen of Columbia University in New York presented the first evidence for ocean rifts. At the end of his lecture in the geology department at Princeton University, the department chairman, Dr. Harry H. Hess, made some summary comments. He basically said, "You have shaken the foundations of geology." Dr. Hess was right.

CHAPTER 2
HOW DO WE KNOW THE CONTINENTS MOVE?

> But still it moves.
>
> —Attributed to Galileo

An Australian graduate student was studying a campsite where some aborigines had lived long ago. At the site, he found a fireplace where the people had cooked. He collected several stones, after carefully recording their position. When he measured magnetism in the stones to find out which direction was magnetic north, he discovered that the Earth's magnetic field was exactly opposite to the way it is today! As recently as 30,000 years ago, magnetic north was toward the South Pole.

Changes in the Earth's magnetic field are a major clue to how the tectonic plates move across the Earth's surface. These changes also let scientists measure how fast the plates move and in what direction they travel. Magnetism is just one part of geophysics, the branch of geology that specializes in the physics of the Earth and its processes.

THE EARTH AS A MAGNET

As new crust forms at the spreading centers on the ocean floor, the rocks record the direction to the north magnetic pole at that moment. This record of the Earth's past magnetic field is called **paleomagnetism.**

For periods of about 500,000 years, the Earth's magnetic field is dominantly of one **polarity,** with the north magnetic pole staying in the same general direction. During this time, many shorter reversals can occur, but magnetic north stays in the same direction most of the time. In a magnetic reversal, a magnetic compass needle changes directions and points "south" instead of "north"—or vice versa. The Earth does not change its position; only the direction to magnetic north changes. Magnetic reversals do not happen overnight. A reversal takes hundreds or thousands of years, and the cause is not known.

The source of the Earth's magnetic field seems to be the fluid outer core of the Earth moving around the solid inner core. The Earth's magnetic field is important because it prevents particles and radiation from the Sun from reaching the Earth's surface—and anything living on the surface. The Earth's magnetic field has been getting weaker for the last several centuries, and this may indicate that another reversal will occur in the next few thousand years.

WHICH WAY IS NORTH?

In 1955, the U.S. Coast and Geodetic Survey was mapping the floor of the Pacific Ocean. The survey contacted a group of scientists at Scripps Institution of Oceanography in California and offered to tow a **magnetometer.** This instrument could record the strength of the magnetism in the ocean crust. The Survey was willing to do this only if the Scripps scientists "did not interfere with their work." The scientists agreed.

When they studied the magnetic patterns on the sea floor, the scientists at Scripps were surprised to discover a series of stripes, with alternating high and low magnetic intensity, parallel to the ocean ridges. Arthur Raff, who had designed the magnetometer, reported. "A single glance [at the data] was enough to know that we had something quite new in geophysics."

The interpretation of these stripes came in 1963, from geophysicists Fred Vine and D. H. Matthews. They knew that basalt was an igneous rock that contained iron-bearing minerals; as basalt cools, it becomes weakly magnetized by the Earth's magnetic field at that moment. The parallel stripes that had been observed on the ocean floor formed as magma cooled, recording the magnetic field. Vine and Matthews suggested that the newly formed rocks attached to the spreading plates and were carried outward in both directions, away from the mid-ocean ridge. New basalt is constantly being added to the plate edges along the rift zone. The importance of these patterns has led geophysicists to call the sea floor a "magnetic tape recorder." The ages of the rocks can be determined with **radiometric dating,** using natural radioactive elements in the rocks. The radioactive material breaks down at a known rate, and this can be used to calculate the age of the rock. From this information, a detailed history of sea-floor spreading can be determined.

As the plates move across the Earth's surface, their relationship to the north magnetic pole changes also. This makes the north pole *appear* to have moved across the Earth's surface. In fact, the magnetic poles change their position only slightly around the two geographic poles; through geologic time, the lithospheric plates have moved relative to the poles. This information has helped scientists reconstruct the locations of the continents and plates earlier in Earth history.

HOW FAST DO THE PLATES MOVE?

Geologists have been able to calculate how fast the plates move, using the magnetic stripes on the ocean floor. They find the place on the ocean floor that records the last magnetic reversal. The age of these rocks tells how long ago the reversal happened. The distance of this spot from the current spreading center shows how much the crust has moved in that time. The rate is given in inches or centimeters per year.

An average rate of plate movement is about 1 inch (2.5 centimeters, or cm) per year. For comparison, this is about as fast as most people's fingernails grow. Although 1 inch per year seems slow compared with the speeds at which people travel, the total movement of the plates, added up over geologic time, has resulted in dramatic changes on the Earth's surface.

Not all the plates are moving at the same speed. The highest plate velocity recorded is between the Pacific Plate and the Nazca Plate, which lies under the southeast Pacific, off the west coast of South America. There, the plates are moving away from the spreading center at 7.2 inches per year (18.3 cm per year).

The rates of movement calculated from magnetic stripes are, of course, long-term averages. The rates vary from place to place and time to time. Some geologists believe that plate speed has been increasing over the past one million years. Now, space age technology is making it possible to determine the rates of motion in great detail. In the near future, laser beams will be bounced off satellites in Earth orbit to measure tiny movements of the Earth's crust. Other new geologic techniques available with satellites are considered in Chapter 11.

HOT SPOTS

Geologists still do not have a clear understanding of what the forces are that push or pull the lithospheric plates, making them move across the Earth's surface. One possible answer is that the movement is caused by narrow columns of hot magma that rise from the mantle. When these reach the surface, they spread outward at places called **hot spots.** Some of the largest hot spots are shown on the world map in Figure 6. These places on the Earth's surface have high temperatures, but their role in pushing—or pulling—plates is still not known.

Where a hot spot occurs at a spreading center, the hot rising magma may push the plates apart. For example, active volcanoes mark the place in Iceland where the American and Eurasian plates are moving apart. A hot spot may lie underneath Iceland, causing both the volcanoes and the plate movement.

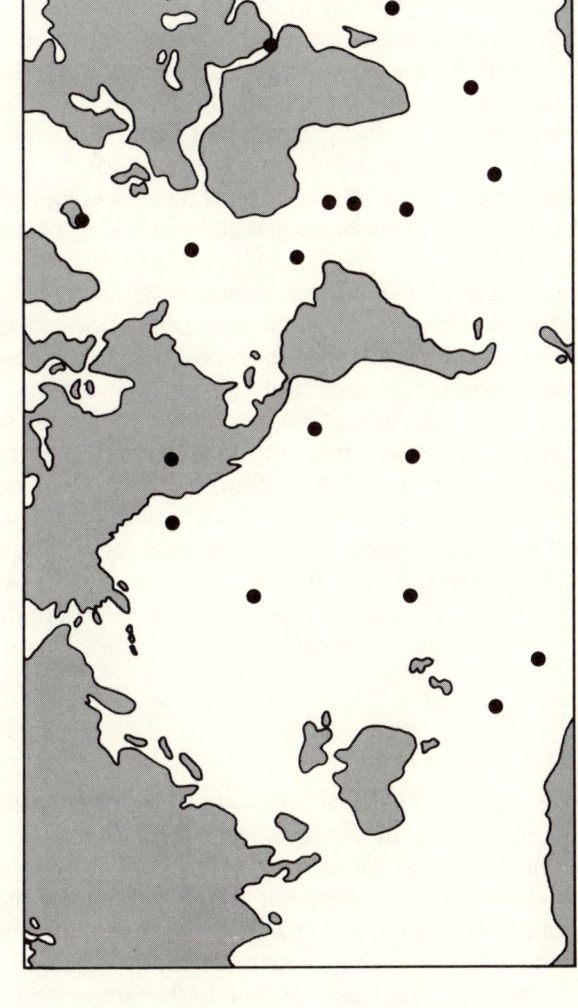

Figure 6. Hot spots are places where mantle rocks are rising to the Earth's surface; they may be a factor in causing plate movement. About twenty of the major hot spots are shown on this map.

If a hot spot is under a continent, volcanoes and hot springs can be expected. One area that may be affected by a hot spot is around Yellowstone National Park in northwestern Wyoming. A hot spot would explain many characteristics of the area, including the geysers, hot ground temperatures, and evidence of volcanic activity in the recent past.

Where a hot spot occurs under the ocean, a string of volcanoes can form. As the oceanic plate moves over the hot magma, the magma punches through to the ocean floor. The volcanoes are then carried away as the plate continues moving, and new volcanoes can form over the hot spot.

If this theory is correct, then the farther away a volcano is from the hot spot (where eruptions are actively taking place), the older it should be.

A good example of this is the Hawaiian Islands in the middle of the Pacific Ocean. The volcanoes active now are on the island of Hawaii, at the southeast end of the island chain. Toward the northwest, the lava that formed the islands is increasingly older. The volcanoes actually continue far across the Pacific, below sea level, in the Hawaiian-Emperor seamount chain. A seamount is a volcano on the ocean floor whose peak is below sea level. Some of these volcanoes never erupted enough to grow above sea level; others have been eroded by waves. In the future, volcanic activity will probably shift farther southeast as the Pacific Plate continues moving slowly to the northwest.

THE GROWTH OF CONTINENTS

Plate tectonics on Earth hasn't always been the same throughout geologic time. In the early Precambrian era—the part of geologic time that includes the first nine-tenths of Earth history—Earth was still very hot. Many radioactive elements were breaking down and giving off energy, and this helped keep the Earth's interior warm for many millions of years after it formed. Because of the high temperatures inside the Earth, plates may have moved much faster across the face of the Earth.

Continents can grow by adding new material to their

edges. The additions can come from volcanic activity or collisions between two smaller land masses. The early Earth may have been covered by many small continents, or microcontinents, perhaps like New Zealand is today. The crashes between these microcontinents would have formed mountain ranges and increased the size of the continents as the smaller pieces were stuck together.

The formation of the Appalachian Mountains in eastern North America is an example of how a continent grows. A collision happened 250 million years ago, during the Paleozoic era, when the African continent ran into North America. In this crash, the continental crust broke, folded, and was pushed up to form the Appalachians.

Volcanic eruptions and the addition of microcontinents also added to the western part of North America over the past 250 million years, during the Mesozoic and Cenozoic eras.

The continents have a long, complicated history of collisions between small crustal plates early in the history of the Earth. Parts of the western United States, for example, were formed by many small land masses colliding over millions of years. Geologists are only now starting to interpret the history of the continents, but the theory of plate tectonics helps us understand more of our planet's history.

Plate tectonics describes the distribution of major features at the Earth's surface and processes like volcanism and earthquake activity, but the theory still cannot explain the exact *causes* of plate movement. Geologists can only guess about the processes deep in the Earth's mantle that affect the plates at the surface. One day, a new theory may explain geological features even better than plate tectonics does now. If and when geologists find such a theory, it will cause another revolution in geology. For the moment, however, plate tectonics is the best theory available to explain many of the forms and processes we observe on Earth.

CHAPTER 3
EXPLORING
THE OCEAN
FLOOR

*He had bought a large map representing the sea
Without the least vestige of land:
And the crew were much pleased when they found it to be
A map they could all understand.*

—Lewis Carroll
The Hunting of the Snark

If you could look at Earth from somewhere out in space, you might think it was incorrectly named. Nearly three-quarters of the surface is covered by water rather than by land. Perhaps the planet should have been named "Ocean" instead of "Earth." Most of the 71 percent of the Earth beneath the sea was hidden from view until recently, and a real understanding of features and processes on the sea floor is only beginning. Current knowledge of offshore areas has been compared to what was known about the western states and territories just after the Civil War. A lot of research still needs to be done.

NEW VIEWS FROM PLATE TECTONICS

For centuries, scientists believed that the ocean floors contained the oldest rocks on Earth. They assumed that the

—35

ocean basins and continents were formed at the same time as the Earth itself, and that the sea floors were featureless plains that had been slowly filling with sediment since their creation.

Modern evidence shows that even the most ancient sea floor is less than 200 million years old, which is very young compared with the age of the continents, where rocks can be almost 20 times older.

Much of our new understanding about the oceans comes out of the theory of plate tectonics. Tectonic activity happens on the sea floor: subduction zones, spreading centers, and hot spots occur there. Before the theory of plate tectonics, each individual feature had to be explained separately.

For example, the Mariana Trench in the western Pacific and the Aleutian Trench near Alaska are both subduction zones where oceanic crust is diving down into the asthenosphere. Without a general theory to explain what is happening in these areas, the two deep trenches were considered to be two different types of valleys. With plate tectonics, geologists realized that these two trenches were formed by the same processes.

The first research expedition to explore the oceans was the Challenger Expedition (1872–76). However, only modern oceanographic research tools have made extensive deep-sea exploration possible. This includes equipment for drilling into rocks in the ocean bottom and small submersibles, which can take scientists far below the ocean surface to study the sea floor directly.

DEEP-SEA DRILLING

Long before the age of plate tectonics, some scientists knew the importance of studying the ocean floor. In 1881, Charles Darwin, the British naturalist, wrote to a Swiss scientist: "I wish that some doubly-rich millionaire would take it into his head to have borings made in some of the Pacific and Indian atolls [islands], and bring home cores. . . ." Seventy years later, new drilling equipment made exploration possible beneath the surface of the oceans.

The sediments on the sea floor tell the history of the ocean basins. Deep-sea drilling collects samples of the sand

and mud on the ocean floor and brings them to the surface to be studied. Pieces of the crustal rocks underneath the sediments are also collected by drilling.

In many ways, deep-sea research started because of the U. S. space program. How are the sea floor and outer space connected? When the U.S. government started spending billions of dollars on exploring space, some earth scientists asked questions. They wondered why so much money should go toward exploring the Moon, when so little was known about our own planet, especially the ocean floor.

In the 1950s, a group of geologists proposed drilling deep cores into the Earth in a "race to the mantle" that would rival the race into space. This effort was called Project Mohole, after the "Moho," the boundary between the Earth's crust and mantle. The crust is much thinner under the oceans than it is under the continents, and so this project would have tried to drill through the ocean floor. Unfortunately, this ill-fated project had problems ranging from technical difficulties to hints of political bribes, and it was finally canceled in 1966.

However, as Project Mohole began to fade, the Deep Sea Drilling Program (DSDP) became important. In 1963, it began as a joint project of the United States and several other governments, including France, Japan, West Germany, and the Soviet Union. The goal of the DSDP was to learn about the history of the world's oceans.

NEW TECHNOLOGIES
FOR DRILLING

The first problem in deep-sea drilling was how to collect cores from the ocean floor. Scientists needed to drill several miles below the ocean surface, through the sediments and crustal rocks on the ocean floor. They needed a research ship that could stay in one place, in water too deep to drop an anchor. If the ship moved, the drill pipe, which may be several miles long, would snap and the cores would be lost. Researchers also wanted to be able to change drill bits—the jagged tips of the drilling equipment that cut into rocks—and reenter the same drill hole more than 3 miles (5 km) below the ship.

The Glomar *Challenger* solved this problem for the DSDP. This research ship had special equipment for keeping its position, in spite of waves and wind. Special signal beacons were placed on the sea floor near the ship, and an onboard computer could monitor the signals. When the computer detected any movement, it automatically started the necessary engines to keep the ship in its correct position. This development made deep drilling on the ocean floor possible.

The Glomar *Challenger* was retired in November 1983. During the years it was used, it traveled more than 375,000 miles (over 600,000 km) on 96 trips. The DSDP collected many cores of rock and sediment, some of them over a mile long.

Most of the sediments collected from the ocean floor are clay-sized particles and the skeletons of microscopic plants and animals. They contain important information about the history of the Earth's climate, ocean currents, and volcanic activity. In places, the cores included some of the oldest rocks on the ocean floor. Where the sediment had not been disturbed, the cores provide an almost continuous record of sea-floor history for more than 180 million years.

The Deep Sea Drilling Project was followed by the Ocean Drilling Program (ODP) in 1985. The ODP is also an international effort to understand the history of the Earth, as it is recorded in the ocean floor. Participating nations include the United States, Canada, France, West Germany, and Japan; the program is expected to operate until 1995.

To replace the Glomar *Challenger*, the drilling ship for the Ocean Drilling Program is the *JOIDES Resolution* (JOIDES stands for "Joint Oceanographic Institutions Deep Earth Sampling"). The *Resolution* is 470 feet (143 m) long, and it has a six-story scientific laboratory equipped with the most modern computers and microscopes. The drills can collect cores to depths of 32,000 feet (10,000 m) below the surface. Because this ship was built to operate in icy water, it will be able to do the first drilling ever in polar regions. Research visits will study the sea floor near Greenland, Antarctica, and the Mid-Atlantic Ridge.

The Glomar Pacific, *a sister ship to the Glomar* Challenger *described in the text, was the first ship to drill into the sediments of the outer continental shelf in the Atlantic Ocean.*

The U.S. Geological Survey collects piston cores from the research vessel Sounder to study sediments in the Gulf of Alaska.

SUBMERSIBLES

Imagine you are in a helicopter, exploring the Grand Canyon in the middle of the night. A blizzard outside keeps your lights from shining more than 15 or 20 feet (4 or 6 m) ahead of the copter, and you only have a few hours to record your observations.

This gives you an idea of what it would be like to study the ocean floor in a submersible. Despite the limitations, manned submersibles have a huge advantage over other types of sea-floor exploration. These tiny submarines allow scientists to study features too small to show up in observations from research vessels. Small submersibles can hold a crew member and one or two scientists. Larger ones may carry a five-person crew to depths as much as 6,500 feet (2,000 m) below sea level.

The equipment on a submersible includes lights, cameras, and mechanical arms to collect samples of the ocean floor. Other instruments can measure the slope of the sediments and their temperature and other physical properties. Submersibles have already been used to study underwater mineral deposits, submarine canyons, and deep-sea volcanoes.

One of the most remarkable efforts to study the sea floor was the 1973 French-American Mid-Ocean Undersea Study, known by its initials as FAMOUS. Two French submersibles and the *Alvin*, operated by the Woods Hole Oceanographic Institution in Massachusetts, took part. During the FAMOUS project, seven dives took scientists down to study the ocean floor for six to eight hours at a time. They visited the spreading center along the East Pacific Rise, near the mouth of the Gulf of California, and made discoveries that could not have been made without submersibles.

An important discovery during Project FAMOUS was **hydrothermal** vents, openings that release hot water. These hot-water vents erupt like geysers, sending fluid 6 to 15 feet (2 to 5 m) above the ocean floor. Surrounding the vents are deposits of metals, including copper, iron, and zinc, which formed as the hot solution met the cold sea water.

Submersibles are extending the ability of scientists to study the ocean floor. The example shown here is the Hydro-Lab, operated by the National Oceanographic and Atmospheric Administration.

Along the East Pacific Rise, hot springs rich in dissolved minerals shoot upward from vents on the ocean floor, forming plumes or "smokers." The chimney shown here is 18 inches (46 cm) high, but other mineral deposits are 6 to 9 feet (1.8 to 2.7 m) in height. This photo was taken from the submersible Alvin *at a depth of about 1.6 miles (2.6 km).*

The water near the ocean floor is very close to freezing. Because of this, submersibles were designed to protect their occupants from cold on the sea floor, not heat. Many of the hot springs on the ocean floor are "hot" only when compared to the temperature of the water around them. Early measurements from submersibles, in the spring of 1977, found water temperatures up to 68°F (20°C).

Later, in November 1979, the *Alvin* was used to study vents along the East Pacific Rise near the Galapagos Islands. Scientists inside the submersible were shocked to discover the Plexiglas windows were getting soft. They realized that the temperatures near the vents reached 662°F (350°C), and special devices had to be designed to collect samples of this hot fluid. The submersible was never intended for heat: the Plexiglas portholes of the *Alvin*, for example, start getting soft at only 155°F (86°C)!

OTHER DISCOVERIES

Scientists in another research submersible, the *Johnson Sea Link I*, recently discoverd a new species of red algae about 800 feet (270 m) beneath the ocean surface. Only about 0.0005 percent of the surface sunlight reaches that depth; before this discovery, no plants had ever been found growing at depths greater than about 550 feet (180 m). These deep-living organisms can trap sediment; their discovery opens many new possibilities for geologic processes in the ocean.

Scientists on the *Alvin* have also found a community of animals living even deeper in the ocean, among the hydrothermal vents on the sea floor. No one expected to discover creatures living at a depth of more than 2 miles (3 km), where no sunlight reaches. These animals seem to eat bacteria that in turn can digest the sulfur being given off at the mid-ocean vents. This is probably the only ecosystem on Earth not based either directly or indirectly on solar energy.

Without the manned deep-diving equipment, these discoveries might have remained unmade for many years. Despite their usefulness, however, these submersibles often see limited activity because of their cost. The expense of operating some submersibles has been estimated at more than $1,000 per hour of diving time. In spite of the cost, submersibles, along with deep-sea drilling, have opened up a dramatic new world on the ocean floor.

CHAPTER 4
RICHES FROM THE SEA

Go, my sons, buy stout shoes, climb mountains, search the valleys, the deserts, the seashores, and the deep recesses of the earth. Mark well the various kinds of minerals, note their properties and their mode of origin.

—Petrus Severinus

Ocean exploration is not just an effort to understand the history of the sea floor. The ocean basins hold valuable resources on and beneath the sea floor, as well as dissolved in the ocean water. Discovering and mining these resources has been an important factor in ocean exploration.

PETROLEUM RESOURCES

In 1859, when Edwin Drake dug the first oil well in Pennsylvania, he drilled in the easiest place he could find. Oil was seeping out of the ground, and his well simply helped the petroleum escape faster.

Since Drake's time, oil companies have always looked for the easiest—and least expensive—way to pump the largest amounts of oil and gas. Because of the difficulties of drilling into the ocean floor, oil exploration and pumping have traditionally been done on land.

As oil and gas become harder to find, exploration has naturally shifted to the oceans. Currently, about one-sixth of the U.S. oil production is collected from drilling platforms that sit on the shallow continental shelf. As these resources near the coastline become depleted, exploration for oil and gas is moving to the deeper oceans. Offshore wells are five to six times more expensive than those on land, and this cost is likely to show up in the future prices of oil and gas to the consumer.

Recent evidence suggests that oil and gas deposits may also occur beneath the deep ocean floor, but drilling in these areas will require some new technological advances. The problems with the drill pipes are obvious; they extend through miles of sea water before reaching the ocean floor. Some scientists are concerned that an oil spill in the deep ocean could create serious ecological problems. The possible environmental problems have already been an issue in many areas where offshore drilling has been proposed. For example, federal permits to allow oil exploration in the waters off southern California are controversial.

LUMPS OF METAL

Another valuable resource on the sea floor is **manganese nodules.** These look like small black potatoes scattered on the deep sea floor, especially in the central Pacific. They con-

Manganese nodules offer a rich source of minerals from the ocean floor. This photograph shows nodules at a depth of about 3 miles (5 km) in the Pacific Ocean near the equator. The small instrument shown here measures the velocity of water moving past the area.

—48

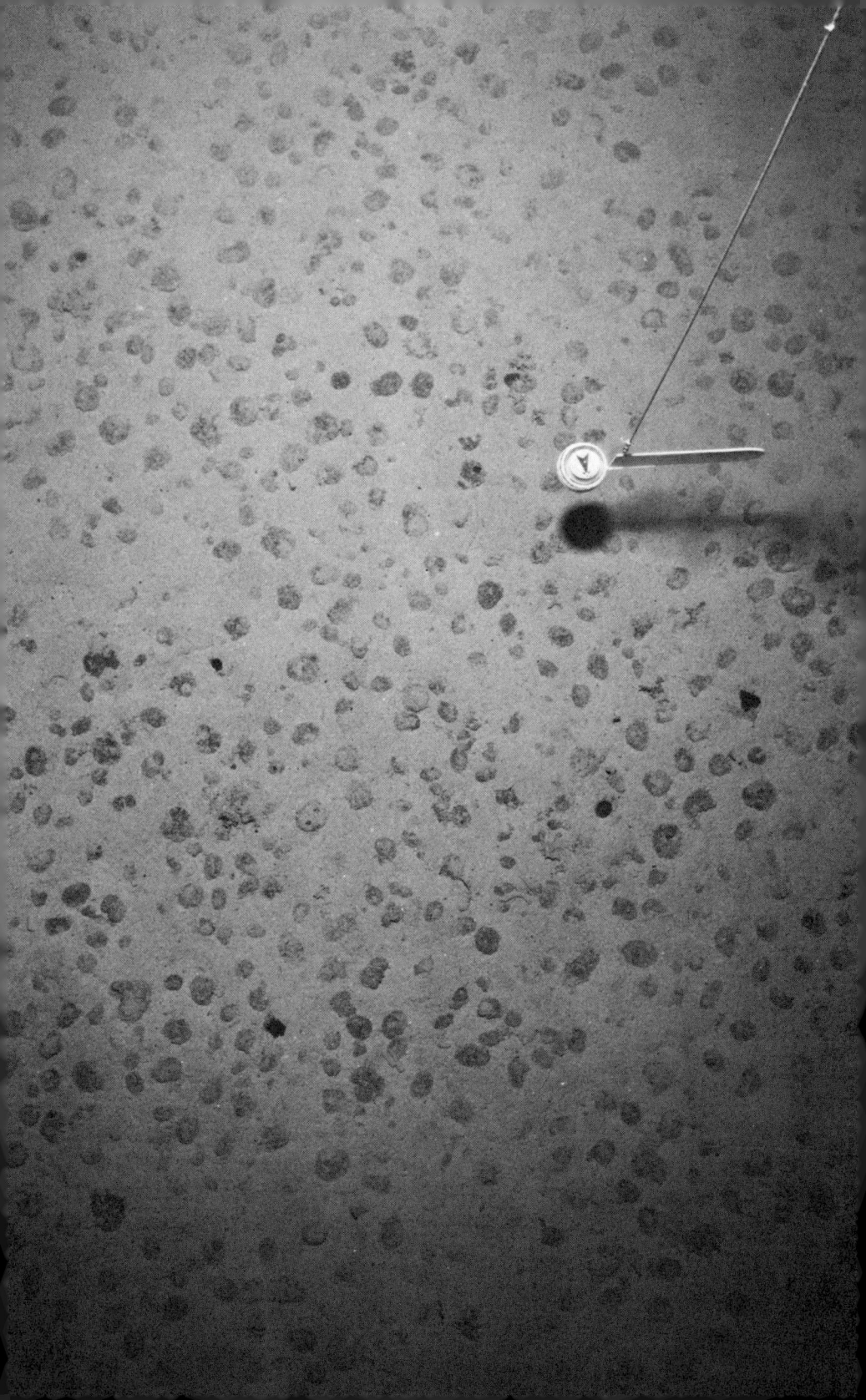

tain large amounts of metals: approximately 25 percent manganese, 15 percent iron, up to 2 percent copper and nickel, and some cobalt. Their origin is not well understood, although the abundance of organisms in the overlying water seems to affect the growth rate and the composition of the nodules.

The major economic interest in these nodules is for the nickel and copper they contain. The manganese concentration is also valuable to the United States, which imports more than 95 percent of the manganese it uses. This metal is necessary for making steel; up to 30 pounds of manganese (7 kilograms, or kg) are needed per ton of steel, and no substitute has ever been found. Manganese nodules are difficult to collect from the ocean floor, but they are clearly valuable. Many countries would like to profit by mining the nodules from the sea floor.

MINERAL DEPOSITS

Hydrothermal areas associated with spreading centers have deposits rich in copper and zinc. Cold ocean water circulates down to the hot rock forming in the rift zones, and when it heats up, it dissolves elements like manganese, copper, zinc, iron, and silver, just as boiling water dissolves sugar. When the hot, mineral-rich water reaches the sea floor again, it mixes with colder water, and the minerals crystallize. They form columns or "chimneys" of sulfide minerals like the ones shown in the photo on page 49.

Understanding how these deposits form is an important step in mineral exploration. Many valuable mineral deposits found on *land* were probably formed at spreading centers in the ocean.

Although they may seem commonplace, sand and gravel are an important resource from the coastal zone. The largest mining efforts on the shallow sea floor collect sand and gravel. The materials are then used in making concrete and cement, in landfills, and for rebuilding beaches. Sands containing large amounts of the mineral quartz can be used in making glass.

Other resources from the sea are also important. Gold,

diamonds, and metals have been found in the sands on the shallow ocean floor. The Soviet Union has been mining uranium from near-shore sands since 1972. The United States collects iron, platinum, and gold from sand deposits also. Farther from shore, the continental slope is covered with muds that contain copper, zinc, lead, and silver. These are too deep to be mined economically right now, but they may become valuable sources in the future.

Some valuable materials are even dissolved in sea water; besides abundant sodium chloride (table salt), about two-thirds of the world's production of bromine and magnesium comes from ocean water. Bromine is used in many insecticides. Because magnesium is a lightweight metal, it is used in airplanes, spacecraft, and portable tools.

WHO OWNS THE SEA?

The existence of minerals and metals on the sea floor has caused a variety of international legal problems. As the mineral wealth of the oceans is discovered, the question of ownership becomes important.

Every coastal nation has a 200-mile (320-km) Exclusive Economic Zone (EEZ) extending from its coastline. Beyond the EEZ is considered international waters. The EEZ of the United States covers a huge area—3.9 billion acres, about one and two-thirds larger than the U.S. land area *above* sea level. This area contains valuable resources. In addition to manganese nodules, as much as 35 percent of the available oil and gas resources of the United States may lie under its EEZ. Concentrations of heavy minerals like gold and platinum may exist in beach sands and in shallow water.

Most of the oceans' supply of manganese nodules is found in international waters, beyond the EEZ. Developing nations feel they have the same right to these resources as the countries that already have the technology to mine them. These developing countries would like to share the technology and the profits, while nations with more advanced technologies would like to begin mining now for themselves.

A recent attempt to resolve this problem was the United Nations' Law of the Sea Conferences. These meetings tried to create a treaty to govern all deep-ocean exploration. In a way, the ownership of the sea floor is like owning property on the Moon: the rights must be shared by all countries. In 1982, the Law of the Sea treaty stated that manganese nodules belong to all people. The treaty proposed that exploration should be regulated by a UN agency. Mining would be restricted and all profits shared.

Four countries voted against the treaty: West Germany, the Soviet Union, Britain, and the United States. As a result, 60 nations must now vote for the treaty before it becomes law. The current policy in the United States favors commercial mining, and a recent U.S. law allows ocean mining to begin in 1988. Until the international legal questions are answered, large-scale mining of manganese nodules and other materials from the deep-ocean floor will probably not occur.

CHAPTER 5
PREDICTING VOLCANIC ERUPTIONS

Study the past if you would divine the future.

—Confucius

*E*veryone would like to be able to predict the future. The popularity of horoscopes is an example of people's curiosity about "what will happen today"—even though they know the predictions are only invented for the morning newspaper. Geologists, however, are beginning to learn how to predict the future of the Earth.

PREDICTING VOLCANIC ERUPTIONS

Volcanic eruptions and earthquakes are common geologic events, but they do not occur very often on a human time scale. Thus, the opportunities to observe major events are relatively few. Areas that do have continuing volcanic or **seismic (SIGHS-mik) activity** (earthquakes) are watched carefully to gather as much information as possible to help in forecasting future events. Collecting large amounts of information is obviously important; sometimes the significance of the observations becomes clear only *after* an eruption or earthquake occurs. Then scientists can review the data, looking for patterns that may have been clues to the larger event. These patterns may include groups of small earthquakes or other events.

The major clues for predicting volcanic eruptions involve earthquake activity, eruption history, magnetic properties, and tilting of the land surface. This earthquake activity represents the movement of magma, or molten rock, toward the surface. When it reaches the Earth's surface, the magma erupts as a lava flow (like the Hawaiian volcanoes) or in an explosion (like the Cascade volcanoes of the Pacific Northwest). Any active volcano will have at least a few small earthquakes every day, even when it is not actively erupting.

For the past several years, many small earthquakes have been happening in the Mammoth Lakes area of the eastern Sierra Nevada in California. Many geologists interpret these earthquakes as meaning that an eruption will happen in the near future. The earthquakes seem to show that a body of hot magma is slowly pushing its way up toward the surface. The U.S. Geological Survey has officially warned the people who live in the Mammoth Lakes area about the possibility of a future eruption, based on the earthquake activity in the region.

In 1978, Dwight Crandall and Donal Mullineaux of the U.S. Geological Survey forecast that Mount St. Helens was likely to erupt before the year 2000. They based this forecast on the historic patterns of eruptions and the length of time since the last event. The huge eruption that occurred in 1980 showed they were right.

Small changes in the slopes near active volcanoes can also warn of a coming eruption. The accumulation of magma beneath a volcano can push up on the surface and create bulges. The instrument that measures these slope changes is called a tiltmeter; this instrument can meaure changes in slope of less than 1 part per million. This is like being able to measure that a board 1 mile long has been lifted 0.06 inch (or a 1-kilometer-long board is raised 1 millimeter) at one end.

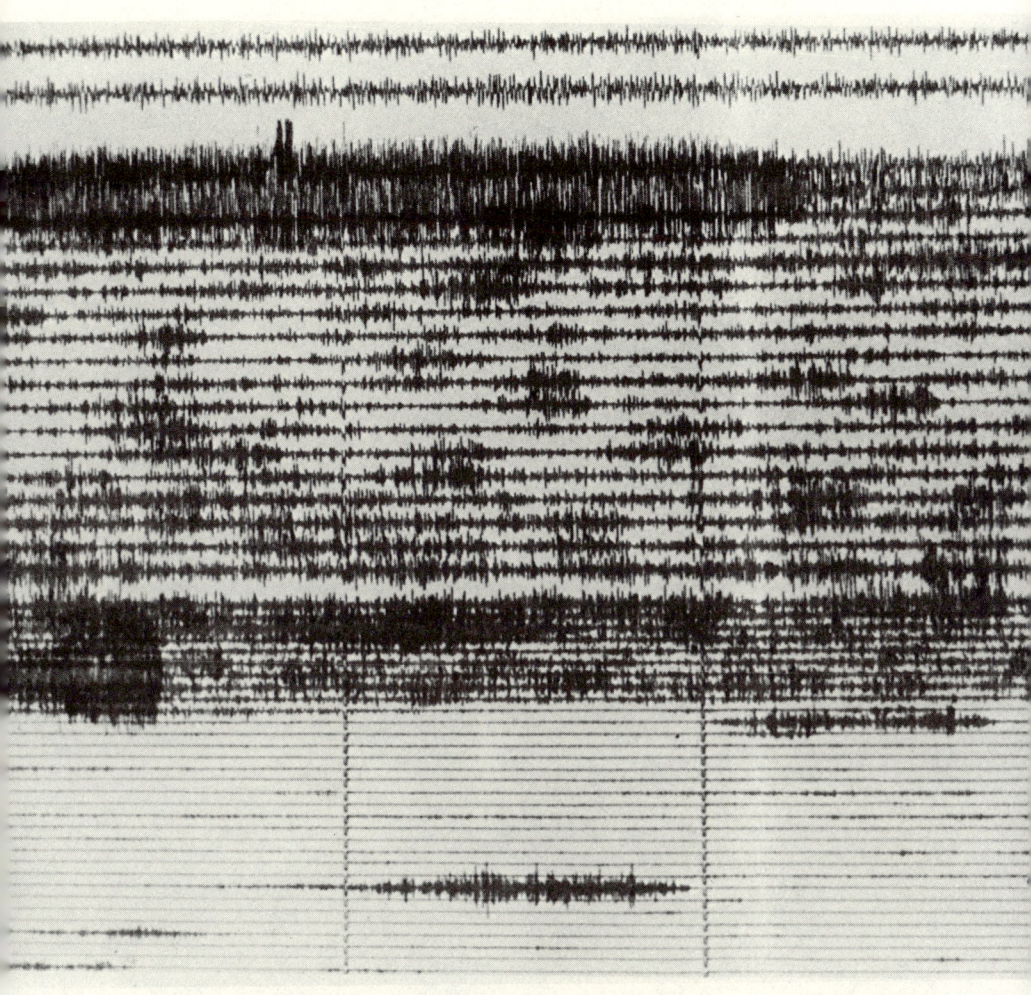

A seismographic record of the July 22, 1980, eruption of Mount St. Helens. A device called a seismograph measures ground vibrations and records them with a special pen on paper. The most intense vibrations produce the greatest movement of the pen, which can be seen here.

In Hawaii, the gases escaping from Kilauea are monitored to determine whether their composition is related to possible future eruptions.

Other observations can also give clues to future eruptions. Changes in the Earth's electrical and magnetic fields just before an eruption have been recorded in New Zealand, Hawaii, Japan, and elsewhere. The types of gases escaping from cracks around volcanoes may also be important; the amounts of sulfur, chloride, hydrogen, helium, and radon all seem to indicate changes in volcanic activity.

SUCCESSES AND FAILURES

No single method can be used by itself to predict volcanic eruptions. The short history of forecasting has examples of both success and failure. For instance, the monitoring of the Hawaiian volcano Mauna Loa began in 1965. When changes in the size of the caldera (crater) at its summit were observed in 1974, geologists warned the public about a possible eruption. As a result, people were reasonably well prepared for the eruptions of July 5 and 6, 1975, when more than 1 billion cubic feet (30 million cubic meters) of lava flowed from the volcano's summit.

Based on the eruption history of Mauna Loa, geologists then predicted that another, possibly more serious, eruption would occur on one of the sides of the volcano before the summer of 1978. This still has not happened. Scientists are still learning about how to make predictions.

In 1975, Soviet scientists observed a major earthquake swarm at the Tolbachik Volcano in Kamchatka, in the U.S.S.R. Geologist P. I. Tokarev predicted—in writing—that the volcano would erupt within a week. When the volcano did erupt two days later, camera crews were in position to record the event. This is the type of precision that geologists would like to have in all their predictions someday.

MOUNT ST. HELENS

The eruption of Mount St. Helens in 1980 was a good illustration of the current state of forecasting of volcanic eruptions. The predictions were reasonably close, but they were not good enough.

Based on the eruption history of the volcano, scientists

with the U.S. Geological Survey had forecast an eruption before the end of the century. They published their conclusions in 1978, just two years before the major eruption of Mount St. Helens. For a geologic event, this was a remarkably accurate forecast.

Beginning in March 1980, other signs pointed toward a coming eruption. These clues included groups of earthquakes, bulging near the volcano's summit, and the concentration of volcanic gases around the volcano. These observations prompted officials to evacuate an area around the volcano. All the residents were warned and asked to leave. Only people on official business were allowed near the volcano.

When Mount St. Helens exploded on May 18, 1980, an area over 200 square miles (500 square kilometers) was blasted by rock and steam. An avalanche moved 15 miles (24 km) down the valley, and the force blew down trees as far as 12 miles (20 km) away.

Evacuation of the area around Mount St. Helens may have saved as many as 30,000 lives. In that respect, the forecast was extremely valuable. However, the eruption on May 18 killed more than 60 people. Nearly all of these people were in the evacuated area. Some were homeowners who had refused to leave. Some "volcano watchers" had entered illegally around barriers and roadblocks. Several were loggers or scientists, like geologist David Johnston, whose duties had taken them close to the mountain that morning. If the eruption's time and intensity could have been predicted more accurately, these people would have been saved, too. This is the current goal of the effort to predict eruptions.

Studies of Mount St. Helens in the years after the May 1980 eruption have given geologists a much better understanding of many volcanic features. The large volcanic landslides at Mount St. Helens are one example. Based on studies there, geologists have identified more than 100 other geologically recent volcanic landslides around the world.

Perhaps the most important fact is that all but a few eruptions of Mount St. Helens *since* May 1980 have been predicted with warning times ranging from three weeks to several hours. Based on what is known about the last major series of eruptions at Mount St. Helens in 1800–57, its current activity can be expected to continue for several decades.

The May 18, 1980, eruption of Mount St. Helens had been predicted by geologists, and as a result relatively few lives were lost.

HAZARDS OF PREDICTION

Trying to predict events like volcanic eruptions and earthquakes has hazards of its own. Along with the possibility of saving lives with a correct forecast, damage can also be done by an incorrect prediction. Problems range from alarming the public unnecessarily to hurting property values and causing economic disaster. The negative impact on public reaction to future predictions must also be considered. The parable of "crying wolf" applies to geologic hazards; after a few false alarms, people will no longer take a prediction seriously.

A recent example of this problem happened on the French island of Guadeloupe in the Caribbean. The volcano La Soufriere has a history of eruptions that end in deadly clouds of hot volcanic ash and gas. When the volcano experienced a small eruption in 1976, officials evacuated 74,000 residents to protect them from the predicted disaster. The explosive ash clouds never developed, and the geologists were blamed for a false alarm.

Another place affected by volcano warnings is the town of Mammoth Lakes, California. Some people were frightened when the U.S. Geological Survey issued its first warnings of possible volcanic eruptions in the area. The popular ski resorts in that region have lost considerable revenue from tourism. As time has passed without an eruption, however, people have stopped worrying, and now they mostly ignore the hazard.

The impact of a predicted hazard isn't always bad. Since the eruption of Mount St. Helens in 1980, each new report of increased seismic activity and possible eruptions brings lots of tourists *to* northwestern Oregon, hoping to see the mountain "blow its top."

CHAPTER 6
UNDERSTANDING EARTHQUAKES

The history of any one part of the earth consists of long periods of boredom and short periods of terror.

—D. V. Ager

The city woke up to a violent shaking. Furniture was lifted up in the air, and people were tossed from their beds. Buildings crumbled, and fires started in the broken gas lines. Because the water lines were broken, too, the fire department couldn't fight the flames. By the time the fires had finally been put out, days later, the city had lost 700 people and hundreds of millions of dollars in property. The fault running under the city had shifted as much as 20 feet (7 m) in places.

The time: 5:12 A.M., April 18, 1906. The place: San Francisco, California. The duration of the earthquake: one minute.

EARTHQUAKES AND
PLATE TECTONICS

Every year, about 500,000 earthquakes are recorded by instruments. Of these, only about 50,000 can be felt by people, and only 100 are classified as strong. Just one or two are severe enough to cause widespread destruction like the one described on the previous page.

Earthquakes affect a far greater number of people than volcanic eruptions. Geologists estimate that between 1900 and 1968 earthquakes caused the deaths of about 800,000 people (1,500 in the United States). Property damage over the same length of time was around $10 billion. Many of the deaths were not caused directly by the quakes, but by fires, landslides, collapsed buildings, and huge sea waves.

Earthquakes are also harder to forecast than volcanic eruptions. Seismology is the study of earthquakes (seismic activity) and the Earth's interior; scientists involved in this subject are trying to learn more about how to predict these events.

If geologists could predict exactly where and when earthquakes will happen, there would be several valuable results. Not only would the predictions save lives and property, but they would also add valuable information to the understanding of plate tectonics. Earthquakes are the vibrations that happen when two rock masses grind past each other, and plate movement is a good example of this. The Earth is adjusting to the stresses caused by tectonic movement.

HOW TO PREDICT AN EARTHQUAKE

Many possible clues to future earthquake activity have been suggested. Some of the more promising ways to predict earthquakes include both short-term and long-range information. The clues that appear shortly before an earthquake include:

1. Changes in seismic velocity. The speed with which vibrations (from faraway earthquakes or ones created artificially, by explosions) travel through the Earth drops before an earthquake. This can happen years before the quake occurs, and then the speed slowly increases until the time the earthquake actually happens. Just before the shake itself, the speed at which the vibrations travel through the Earth returns to normal.

A geologist checks her recording station along the San Andreas Fault in southern California. The water level in wells may prove to be an important indication of a coming earthquake.

2. Changes in the water level in wells. Before an earthquake occurs, stresses in the rocks can squeeze or expand the openings that contain water, changing the water level in wells. These same forces may also explain the changes in types and amounts of gases in well water that happen just before an earthquake.

3. Unusual animal behavior. No one has found a good explanation for the strange actions of animals just before a quake, but they have been recorded so often that they cannot be ignored. Reported examples include snakes coming out of their hiding places in freezing weather, chickens coming home to roost, and house pets behaving in unusual ways. Suggested explanations include the animals' ability to "hear" an earthquake coming, changes in atmospheric gases, and fluctuations in the local magnetic or gravitational field. None of these has ever been proven to be the cause.

Other clues for predicting earthquakes are based on historical records. Such long-term warnings of a future earthquake include:

1. Relatively regular cycles of activity. Some recent studies of fault zones have shown the history of movements in those areas. These studies use deep trenches dug across the fault, and they show that the rocks along some faults move at fairly regular intervals.

Geologist Kerry Sieh, at the California Institute of Technology in Pasadena, has found that great earthquakes have happened along the San Andreas fault near Los Angeles at intervals of about 150 years. The last movement of the San Andreas in that area was in 1857, and the probability of a major earthquake in the next 30 years is very high.

2. The "seismic gap theory." A seismic gap is a section along an active fault that has not had any recent activity—and therefore is due for an earthquake. Many long faults, like the San Andreas in California, have some parts that are sliding smoothly past each other with little earthquake activity. These are called "creep zones." Other areas, the "locked

zones," are not moving. These zones seem to be building up energy that will later be released, all at once, in a large earthquake.

According to the seismic gap theory, faults where no earthquakes have happened for a long time are exactly the areas most likely to have a major earthquake in the future. This theory is directly related to plate tectonics. Because the whole plate is moving, rocks on both sides of the fault must be moving past each other. In some places, the rocks slide smoothly. In other places, the rocks "stick" and stresses build up until they are released violently. These earthquakes are usually dangerous and cause a lot of damage.

The seismic gap theory has already been proven correct by recent earthquakes in China and Alaska. In China, especially, many lives have been saved by successful predictions of seismic gaps. Along the San Andreas fault, both San Francisco and Los Angeles are in locked zones, with creep zones on either side of them. This points toward the likelihood of a large earthquake striking these cities in the near future.

THE PARKFIELD PREDICTION

In April 1985, the U.S. Geological Survey (USGS) gave its first official endorsement to an earthquake forecast. Geologists at the University of California at Berkeley and the USGS had studied earthquakes along the San Andreas near the town of Parkfield, California. They found these earthquakes happened at approximately 22-year intervals, with similar patterns of movement each time. The last event was in 1966, so the geologists concluded another earthquake was likely soon. They predicted an earthquake strong enough to knock down poorly constructed buildings would occur before 1993.

This predicted earthquake would be too small to cause much damage, but a correct forecast would be a major advance for seismology as a science. This prediction, if it is successful, should help make similar forecasts in other areas possible. It also helps geologists know where to concentrate their recording equipment so that they can measure and record the earthquake—when it happens—in the most effective way.

Any prediction of an earthquake is evaluated carefully before it becomes official. In 1977, the United States Congress established the National Earthquake Prediction Evaluation Council to advise the U.S. Geological Survey. Only one other forecast, for two major earthquakes in Peru, had been submitted to the Council, and that was rejected in 1981. California also has a similar advisory body, and this group has also endorsed the Parkfield prediction.

DO-IT-YOURSELF EARTHQUAKES

Between 1962 and 1966, the U.S. Army pumped waste water deep into the ground at its Rocky Mountain Arsenal, east of Denver, Colorado. Hundreds of small earthquakes were recorded in the area. Geologists eventually realized that the additional water pressure was pushing the rocks on both sides of the fault apart. As a result, earthquakes were happening as the rocks slipped past each other.

This accidental discovery showed geologists that they might be able to *cause* earthquakes. In 1970, experiments were done in the Rangely oil field in northwest Colorado. These showed that earthquakes could be started—and stopped—by pumping water in or out of the ground.

Based on these discoveries, some geologists hope that one day it may be possible to prevent major earthquakes by triggering a series of smaller ones on purpose. Certainly a series of small jerks—and minor earthquakes—would be safer than one major quake. Experiments with this need to be done when the stresses across the fault are low. As geologist M. King Hubbert has pointed out, "If you're going to mess with a mousetrap, mess with it when it's not set!"

"Earthquake engineering" will be a true revolution in geology when it becomes possible.

CHAPTER 7
WHAT KILLED THE DINOSAURS?

In the fight for survival, a tie or split decision simply will not do.

—Merle L. Meacham

Who hasn't been interested in dinosaurs? These huge, burly creatures—some friendly, some ferocious—have captured people's imaginations for hundreds of years. Dinosaurs ruled the Earth during the Mesozoic (MEZ-o-ZOH-ik) era of geologic time, which lasted from 225 to 65 million years ago. These giant reptiles have populated science fiction, horror films, and gasoline advertisements. They clearly ruled the world around them, but all the dinosaurs disappeared from Earth about 65 million years ago, at the end of the geologic period called the Cretaceous (cree-TAY-shus). Why?

The history of life on Earth records several episodes of **mass extinction,** when many plants and animals died. In the most dramatic of these, more than half of all species then living disappeared, including all the dinosaurs. The mass extinction that happened 65 million years ago is sometimes called the Cretaceous/Tertiary (TER-sher-ee) extinction, after the periods in geologic time that are separated by this event.

—67

Until recently, no one had a good response to the question "What killed the dinosaurs?" Many theories had been proposed, but none had been widely accepted. Now, a revolutionary new idea may provide the answer.

POSSIBLE CAUSES

Theories for mass extinctions have ranged from very specific to very general ones. The specific explanations for why the dinosaurs died include the following: mammals ate all the dinosaur eggs; the dinosaurs became too "stupid" to survive; and the dinosaurs ate all their available food supplies.

Obviously, these only explain the disappearance of the dinosaurs, not what happened to all the other species of animals and plants that died out at the same time. More general theories are needed to explain the disappearance of large groups of organisms. These causes include worldwide climatic change, deadly radiation from exploding stars, and widespread disease. Recently, a theory has emerged that may explain the extinctions that occurred 65 million years ago, as well as other extinctions in Earth history.

The story of the new theory starts in a lab in Berkeley, California, where scientists were studying a sample of clay that was 65 million years old. This clay had been collected near the Italian village of Gubbio, and the scientists were interested in finding out what elements the clay contained. The thin clay layer, which marks the boundary between the Cretaceous and Tertiary periods, is different from the rock above and below it. The existence of clay means that very fine-grained material (like dust or silt) was deposited then, and later it was compressed into rock.

To their great surprise, the researchers discovered that this clay had large amounts of several "noble" elements. This group is composed of metals that are chemically very stable. The most significant of these are the elements iridium and platinum, and they also include gold and osmium. The concentration of these elements in the clay layer was 100 times or more greater than normal occurrences on Earth.

Where could these unusual elements have come from? The scientists, led by Luis and Walter Alvarez, realized that

comets and **asteroids** have as much as 10,000 times the concentration of these elements as the Earth's surface. Both of these types of planetary bodies are probably left over from the early formation of the Solar System. Comets are mostly frozen gas and dust, while asteroids are small and rocky. Either of these would be a good source for the iridium and platinum in the clay layers deposited 65 million years ago. Based on this evidence, the Alvarezes proposed that an asteroid or comet, probably about 6 miles (10 km) in diameter, hit the Earth about 65 million years ago.

This collision would have created a huge explosion and a crater nearly 90 miles (150 km) across. Some of the earth material would have been thrown high into the atmosphere as dust. Because 71 percent of the Earth's surface is covered by water, chances are good that this object would have hit the ocean, which may explain why no one has found a large crater 65 million years old.

If the asteroid or comet hit the ocean, the effect of the impact is unchanged; hitting the ocean only means that the impact would have thrown more water vapor into the atmosphere, along with the dust. The recent discovery of soot in this clay layer suggests that large fires might also have been started by the impact.

BLOCKING THE SUNLIGHT

The cloud of dust and water vapor tossed into the atmosphere would have hidden the Earth's surface from sunlight, perhaps for months. Green plants, which need light to photosynthesize and produce their own food, would have died fairly quickly. This would include everything, from flowering plants and pine trees to the microscopic organisms in the ocean. As plants died, on land and in the ocean, the animals that needed them for food would also begin to starve. These would be followed by the animals that ate the plant-eating animals, and so on up through the food chain. Ultimately, all animals depend on plants (directly or indirectly), and so the lack of sunlight for photosynthesis would be a problem for animals as well as plants.

The huge dust clouds in the atmosphere would also have shaded the Earth's surface, causing it to cool. Temperatures might even have fallen below freezing in some places. Some smaller land animals, like mammals, might have been able to find burrows and shelters to hide in. The larger creatures, however, including the dinosaurs, would not have been able to find cover so easily. Hit by both cold temperatures and a lack of food, many organisms would have died.

Paleontologists, the geologists who study the history of life on Earth, don't know how long this dust cloud may have lasted and how cold the Earth may have become. Based on what is known about the atmosphere today, scientists think the dust cloud may have darkened the sky for more than a year. By the time the dust cleared and sunlight fell on the Earth's surface again, more than half of the species that had lived in the late Cretaceous period would have disappeared. This would have included all the dinosaurs, many flowering plants, and numerous other organisms that lived on land. It also would have included 95 percent of the invertebrate species that lived in the seas.

OTHER EVIDENCE

At nearly 50 sites around the world, rocks can be found that are 65 million years old. These were probably deposited just at the time that the mass extinctions occurred. In all but two of these clay layers, the rocks have high concentrations of the noble elements, especially iridium. The most studied location where this 65-million-year-old "boundary clay" occurs is near the Italian village of Gubbio. This is the clay layer Walter and Luis Alvarez were studying when they proposed their theory.

The iridium-rich clay layer is less than an inch thick and underlain by a limestone that was deposited in deep water. This limestone is filled with fossils of the life that filled the late Mesozoic seas, including many one-celled organisms. Twenty species of foraminifera, a one-celled animal about 1/16 inch (1.5 millimeters, or mm) across, can be found just below the clay layer. Only one of these animal species is found in the limestone above the clay layer. The other 19 species died in

The Morrison Formation in Wyoming is a rich source of dinosaur bones recording the mass extinction that occurred 65 million years ago.

the mass extinction. The event that caused the extinctions may have been even more destructive to life in the oceans than it was to life on land, where the dinosaurs ruled.

COMET OR ASTEROID?

This theory for the Cretaceous extinctions is often called "the Asteroid and the Dinosaur Theory," but the impact could also have been caused by a comet. Both asteroids and comets were formed at the birth of the Solar System. They also contain the elements concentrated in the clay layer separating Cretaceous and Tertiary rocks. However, comets and asteroids have many differences.

Asteroids are large chunks of rock that can be considered minor planets. They range in size from less than 1 mile (1.6 km) to several hundred miles (up to 1 thousand km) across. If all of the 100,000 known asteroids were lumped together, their total mass would be less than that of Earth's Moon. Most of them orbit the Sun in a region between Mars and Jupiter, in a zone called the asteroid belt. A few groups, however, have regular orbits that cross the Earth's.

For obvious reasons, scientists are interested in identifying those asteroids whose orbits cross Earth's path. The immediate effects of an asteroid impact would probably be similar to those of a nuclear explosion, and *all* nations would want to know that the explosion was a natural event and not the beginning of a world war. It is no surprise that the U.S. Department of Defense sponsors many of the Earth-crossing asteroid studies in the United States.

Comets are balls of ice and dust that have been described as "dirty snowballs." This ice is composed of water and other materials that are liquid or gas on Earth, but frozen solid at the cold temperatures of outer space.

Most comets circle the Sun in an orbit far beyond Pluto, in a region that extends out to about 50,000 **astronomical units** (A.U.). One A.U. is the mean distance between the Earth and the Sun, about 93 million miles (150 million km). The region where most comets are found is called the Oort cloud, after the Dutch astronomer Jan Oort.

Comets can be pulled out of the Oort cloud by the gravity of passing stars. This gravitational tug starts the comet in an orbit around the Sun. As a comet gets closer to the Sun, solar heat begins to vaporize some of the ice in the comet. These gas and dust particles form the "tail" of the comet as they stream away from the Sun. The length of time a comet takes to complete one orbit around the Sun ranges from as little as three years to more than 80,000 years. The familiar Halley's Comet takes between 74 to 79 years, but it never goes all the way out to the Oort cloud.

A comet would hit the Earth with a speed of about 25 miles per second (40 km per second), about twice as fast as an asteroid. This may seem like a large difference, but it isn't really very important. Dr. Eugene Shoemaker of the U.S. Geological Survey, who has studied impact craters on Earth for many years, says that both asteroids and comets would be going so fast when they hit the Earth that "it wouldn't matter whether it's made of ball bearings or custard pie—the final crater would be the same."

Whether a comet or an asteroid hit the Earth 65 million years ago, the crater and type of particle that would be thrown into the atmosphere would be roughly the same. The dust particles that would form the clay layers might be different, but no clues have yet been found to tell whether the impact was made by an asteroid or a comet. The major argument for an asteroid is simply that, through geologic time, asteroids have hit the Earth twice as often as comets. As a result, most scientists who support the Alvarez' theory speak of an asteroid that hit the Earth 65 million years ago, but the impact could just as easily have been from a comet.

UNDERSTANDING THE PAST AND FUTURE

The disappearance of the dinosaurs remains one of the greatest mysteries in Earth history. A collision between Earth and an asteroid or comet explains many observations, including the clay layers, the elements they contain, and the global effect on life. However, many questions must still be answered before an impact theory becomes widely accepted. Why did some species (especially mammals) survive the cold and dark? How long did the effects of a global dust cloud last? Where is the crater formed by the impact?

Studies of the possible effects of an asteroid impact have already been important outside of traditional geology. The dust thrown into the atmosphere probably resembles the dust and ash that would be formed by a large nuclear explosion. The ash and dust would absorb incoming sunlight, lowering temperatures around the world. This cold, dark time predicted to follow a major bomb blast has been called "nuclear winter," and it would be very similar to the freezing darkness caused by a major asteroid or comet impact. In both cases, tiny particles in the atmosphere would block out sunlight. Because plants could no longer carry out photosynthesis, they would die, and the animals that eat the plants would also die.

The geologic past may have useful lessons for the future of modern society. Whatever caused their extinction, the dinosaurs had no choice in their future. We do have a choice in ours. We may not control comets and asteroids, but we can influence human events and the prospects for world peace. Perhaps, in doing so, we may escape the fate of the dinosaurs.

One of the people who studies the causes of mass extinctions is Dr. Stephen Jay Gould, a geologist and paleontologist at Harvard University in Massachusetts. He has pointed out that the disappearance of the dinosaurs made room for the rise of mammals. If the dinosaurs had not died, we would not be here today. Dr. Gould sees an important lesson in that. Most of all, he is impressed "to think that the asteroid or the comets that made our own lives possible may, through the impetus they gave to the development of the scenario of nuclear winter, now help to save us again."

CHAPTER 8
EXPLAINING EXTINCTIONS IN GEOLOGIC HISTORY

The crash of the whole solar and stellar systems could only kill you once.

—Thomas Carlyle

What do dinosaurs and 225-million-year-old clams have in common?

The answer to this question is that they may both have been destroyed by the same type of event—whether it was a collision with a comet, a volcanic eruption, or a change in climate. The mass extinction at the end of the Cretaceous period was the most dramatic in Earth history, partly because it included the dinosaurs. However, it was not the only one that has ever happened. Other episodes of widespread extinctions have occurred at other times in Earth history, including around 37, 225, 345, and 500 million years ago. Figure 7 shows the geologic time scale, including episodes when mass extinctions occurred.

CYCLES OF EXTINCTIONS?

Mass extinctions, like the one that killed the dinosaurs, occur as regular events in Earth history. Over the last 250 million years, extinction episodes may have happened every 26 to 33 million years. This timing is not exact, but studies of the fossil record suggest that there may be cycles approximately that long. Not all geologists, however, believe these cycles occur. Two problems need to be resolved before geologists can prove that extinctions happen at regular intervals.

One common problem affects all research using fossils. The fossil record is not very precise, and exact ages are hard to determine. In some cases, the age estimate has an error of 30 million years. For example, if an extinction episode can be dated only at 200 million years ago plus or minus 30 million years, then it could have occurred at 230 million years ago— or 170 million years ago. This makes specific statements about 30-million-year cycles open to question.

But perhaps the greater problem with proposing these cycles of extinction is the need to explain *why* the cycles are that long. What controls the timing? Eugene Shoemaker, one of the geologists who study these cycles, refers to the controlling factor as the "clock." No processes on Earth have been found that vary regularly on a 30-million-year cycle, although rates of sea-floor spreading and volcanic activity have been suggested. Geologists have now started looking for the answer outside of Earth.

A DEATH STAR?

One of the most interesting suggestions for the "clock" that controls extinctions on Earth is that our Sun has a companion star that comes close to the Sun every 26 million years. This companion star, when it is exactly the right distance from the Sun, would be able to "tickle" the cloud of comets that surrounds the Solar System. The star's gravity would pull a comet out of the cloud and start it flying in toward the Sun. On its way through the Solar System, the comet would cross the orbit of Earth. If conditions were correct, it could hit the Earth, followed by the same chain of events already described. Of course, a companion star would not affect an asteroid, and so it could only cause a collision with a comet.

Such a companion star has never been observed by astronomers, but scientists have calculated what the characteristics of such a companion star would be. The "companion" may ultimately turn out to be a star like our Sun, a smaller and denser type of star called a "black dwarf," or even a large planet with a mass about ten times that of Jupiter.

The prospect for a companion star is not likely, based on information from geophysics. A major problem with this theory is that, if a companion star formed at the same time as our Sun and Solar System, its orbit would have been unstable. Very quickly, the companion would have moved from its original position. Overall, the chances are small that such a star would remain for long in the right location, where it could disturb the comet cloud. Most predictions estimate that this companion star must have an orbit perpendicular to the Earth's orbit around the Sun, beyond the Oort cloud. That is where astronomers are looking now.

Whatever—and wherever—it is, this companion has already been given a name: Nemesis (NEM-eh-sis), after the Greek goddess of doom. The word is used to describe any fierce rival. If Nemesis does exist and is ultimately responsible for causing comets to crash into Earth, then it is a powerful rival indeed. Some recent articles about the possible existence of this companion star have also called it "Death Star."

PLANET X AND OTHER THEORIES

Another theory to explain why comet showers might occur at 30-million-year intervals proposes the existence of a tenth planet. This planet would be beyond the orbit of Pluto, at a distance of about 100 astronomical units from the Sun. Detailed calculations have indicated that a tenth planet with a mass between five and ten times that of Earth would have a major effect on comets. However, the existence of a tenth planet, traditionally called Planet X, cannot explain why comets would fall toward the Earth in regular "showers," rather than at a uniform rate, so this may not offer a complete answer.

Astronomers have searched for a tenth planet since the discovery of Pluto in 1930, always without success. If Planet X exists, it must be very small, very dim, or very far away.

Another explanation for why mass extinctions seem periodic derives from the fact that the entire Solar System moves through the galaxy every 33 million years. As a unit, the Sun and planets move up and down relative to the plane of the galaxy, passing through dust clouds in the process. If this were the cause, however, mass extinctions should be occurring today.

Geologic changes have also been associated with a longer time scale of about 250 million years. Causes of such long-term variations might be magnetic changes, mountain-range formation, changes in sea level, and spreading rates. So far, no one has found a definite explanation for regular cycles of these geologic processes, although some possible answers are discussed in the next section.

OTHER SOURCES OF DUST

The idea that a huge impact would create a worldwide dust cloud has led to other theories as well. After all, Earth has easier ways to put dust into the air than an extraterrestrial impact. Volcanic eruptions are one example of this.

The eruption of Krakatoa in 1883 is an example of a major volcanic eruption. During the volcanic explosions, nearly 5 cubic miles (21 cubic km) of material were thrown high into the atmosphere as dust. This volume would bury nearly 20,000 football fields under a mile of material! Climatic data indicate a slight drop (about 0.5°F, or 0.3°C) in worldwide temperatures for several years after this eruption, caused by the dust blocking out the sunlight. Certainly the spectacular sunsets during the year following the Krakatoa eruption were a result of the scattering of sunlight by dust in the atmosphere.

The largest volcanic eruption in recorded history was the explosion of Mount Tambora in Indonesia in 1815. More than 25 cubic miles (100 cubic km) of ash were thrown high into the atmosphere. Reports say the Sun and stars were darkened in New York, London, and elsewhere around the world. The average temperature in the northern hemisphere dropped more than 1°F (0.7°C) over the following year. In fact, 1816 became known as the "year without a summer."

Daily temperatures were unusually low, rain and snow fell across Europe and North America, and many crops failed. Blocking sunlight by atmospheric dust is not the only explanation for these events, but the dust was almost certainly a factor.

Other examples of the darkening and cooling associated with atmospheric dust have come from very recent volcanic eruptions, including that of El Chichon in Mexico in 1982. The eruption of Mount St. Helens in 1980, despite its dramatic effects, did not produce any noticeable changes in global temperature. However, events like these are important ways to test the dust theory without being able to observe an extraterrestrial impact.

Geologic events like volcanic eruptions may also occur at somewhat regular intervals. Evidence from several areas on Earth supports the possibility of volcanic activity around 65 million years ago. For example, India has a huge lava field that formed 30 to 100 million years ago—but with the greatest activity around 60 to 65 million years ago. Over a 400,000-year period, 240,000 cubic miles (1 million cubic km) of lava flowed onto the surface. (This volume of material would cover the entire state of Texas to a depth of 1 mile, or 1.6 km). These eruptions were relatively quiet, but other, more violent eruptions may have happened at the same time.

The volcanic theory has some strong supporters. One possibility is that the groups believing in the asteroid impact and volcanic eruptions are both correct. Perhaps a huge asteroid or comet also caused widespread volcanic eruptions when it hit the Earth.

DO EXTINCTIONS REALLY HAPPEN AT REGULAR INTERVALS?

The history of life seems to show extinctions at 26- to 33-million-year intervals. However, the geologic record is not precise enough to say this with certainty. In addition, no "clock" has been found to explain *why*. This lack of a good explanation has led many geologists to conclude that there is no clock controlling extinctions on Earth. Mass extinctions may occur as pulses, in random groupings, but not as regular cycles.

Understanding geologic history is valuable for predicting the future. Extinctions continue to occur. For example, the passenger pigeon disappeared in 1914, influenced greatly by human overuse, and the California condor is threatened today. Many other species are endangered. If we understand what causes extinctions, we may be able to help protect some species and prevent a dramatic loss of life forms on Earth. Perhaps most directly, we may be able to prepare the human species for a changing environment—whether caused by global dust clouds, decreasing sunlight, or volcanic eruptions. Certainly this would be a valuable contribution from geology to society.

CHAPTER 9
EXTRATERRESTRIAL GEOLOGY: THE MOON AND BEYOND

It is possible that there is, after all, something unique about man and the planet he inhabits.

—Theodosius G. Dobzhansky

On July 20, 1969, people around the world held their breath as the Apollo 11 astronauts prepared to open the hatch of their lunar module to be the first humans to leave their footprints on the Moon. This event marks a major revolution in geology. For the first time in history, geologists could study rocks that had been collected on another planetary body.

Although "geology" literally means the study of the Earth, Apollo 11 forced geologists to expand the definition. "Lunar geology" was used at first, and now "planetary" and "extraterrestrial" geology are common terms.

The geology of other planetary bodies has caused a revolution in thinking called the "planetary perspective." The most important lessons are the similarities and differences between Earth and the other planets of the Solar System. These other planets give valuable information about Earth, and both the similarities and the differences help us to understand Earth better.

Temperature is a major characteristic that sets Earth apart from any of the other planets. Earth is the only body in our Solar System where the average temperature is between the freezing and boiling points of water (32–212°F, or 0–100°C). The average global temperature on Earth is about 60°F (15°C). Earth stays at this temperature because of its distance from the Sun and energy-absorbing gases in the atmosphere. These gases trap radiation as it leaves the Earth, and this keeps the atmosphere warm. Heating by this blanket of air is called the **greenhouse effect.**

Because of the temperature range, Earth has water in all three of its chemical phases: solid (ice), liquid (water), and gas (water vapor, in the air). The presence of all three phases has important effects on both the erosional processes operating at the surface and on the possibilities for life to exist on the planet. Life can exist on Earth only because of this moderate temperature.

EARTH-LIKE PLANETS

The four inner planets of the Solar System are the **terrestrial planets,** so called because they are Earth-like and have many features in common. Mercury, Venus, Earth (and Moon), and Mars are all relatively small, dense, and rocky. On the terrestrial planets other than Earth, impact craters are the most common surface features. Because our Moon is so large, compared to the size of Earth, it is sometimes included as a terrestrial planet. The Moon is also covered with craters, and its largest ones can be seen from Earth without a telescope. Yet we see few craters on the surface of Earth.

This simple observation points out one of the most important differences between Earth and the other terrestrial

The cratered surface of the Moon shows that little geologic activity is occurring there today. The area shown here is about 110 miles (175 km) across; this television picture was taken about 3 minutes before Ranger IX crashed into the lunar surface.

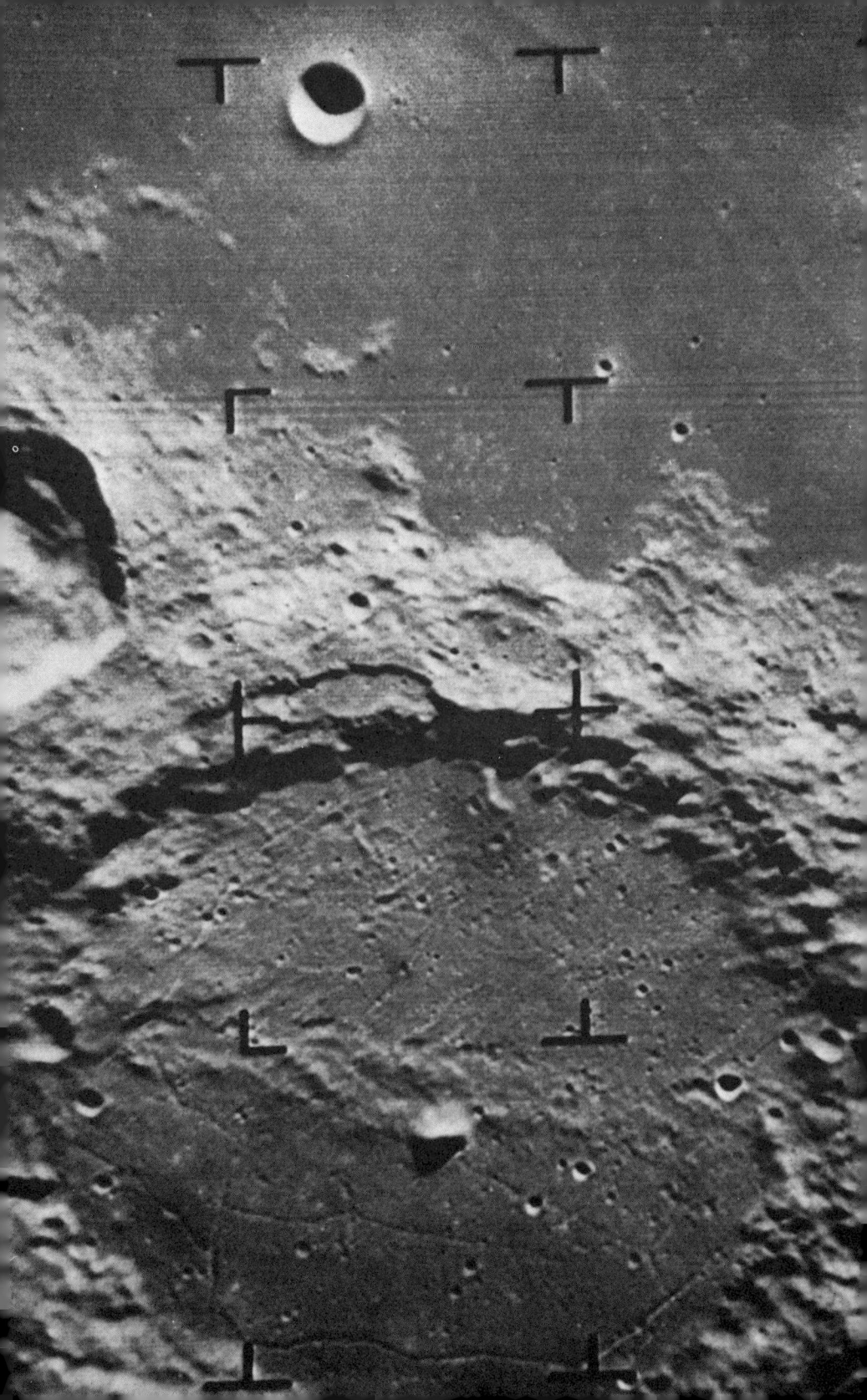

planets. Earth has a dynamic surface. Plate tectonics continually change the Earth's crust, destroying material through subduction, pulling ocean crust down into the Earth's interior, and then creating new crust at volcanoes and mid-ocean ridges. Liquid water flows across the land surfaces in rivers and streams, eroding and wearing down the land. The best example of an impact crater on Earth—Barringer (Meteor) Crater in Arizona—is only 10,000 to 50,000 years old. It has not had time to be completely eroded by the wind and infrequent rainstorms of the desert.

VOLCANOES ON OTHER PLANETS

All the terrestrial planets have some evidence of igneous activity, but the specific types vary greatly. Mercury and the Moon have evidence of very old, fluid lavas that flowed across their surfaces, but the eruptions seem to have stopped around 3.5 to 4 billion years ago. Their surfaces are now heavily pocked with impact craters.

Mars, however, has both small and large volcanoes, including one more than twice the height of the largest volcano known on Earth. The giant Martian volcano Olympus Mons (named after Mount Olympus in Greek mythology—the mountain of the gods) may have erupted as recently as 100,000 years ago. Geologically speaking, a hundred thousand years ago was yesterday. No active eruptions have been observed on Mars, however.

The Pioneer spacecraft that arrived at Venus in 1978 measured the amount of sulfur dioxide in the atmosphere there. Sulfur dioxide is what causes the strong smell when a match is struck, and it can combine with water to form sulfuric acid. This compound had never been detected in Venus' atmosphere before, and the amount has decreased ever since Pioneer's first observation. Some geologists believe the sulfur dioxide was formed by volcanic eruptions on Venus in the late 1970s.

The presence of volcanoes on Venus is still being debated. Only **radar,** which bounces radio signals off the surface, is able to "see through" the dense, cloudy atmosphere.

Radar images suggest that Venus has circular structures, but these might be either craters or volcanic calderas. Lightning storms have also been observed in the atmosphere of Venus. This may be evidence of active volcanic eruptions, but this has not been proven yet.

WIND AND WATER

On planets with atmospheres, wind is an important geologic agent at the surface. Mercury has a very thin atmosphere; the planet is probably too small to hold enough molecules with its gravity to have a real atmosphere. If it once had a thicker atmosphere, the gases probably escaped long ago.

Venus has an atmosphere almost 100 times denser than the Earth's. It is composed mostly of carbon dioxide and clouds of sulfuric acid. The winds are very strong near the cloud tops of Venus, but probably not near the surface. The air on Venus has the eroding ability of the acid found in car batteries.

Earth's atmosphere is composed of 78 percent nitrogen, 21 percent oxygen, and less than 1 percent carbon dioxide, argon, and other gases, including water vapor. Earth may actually have as much carbon dioxide as Venus, but on Earth it is chemically trapped in limestone rocks and dissolved in sea water.

Mars' atmosphere is only about 1 percent as dense as Earth's and is composed mostly of carbon dioxide. On all of the terrestrial planets, except Mercury and the Moon, winds blow across the surface, moving particles and eroding the rocks. Indeed, the fastest wind speeds recorded by the Viking Landers on Mars are even higher than the fastest winds recorded on Earth.

Earth is the only planet whose average temperature falls within the range for liquid water, so it is the only planet that can have rivers and oceans of water. Because of the high temperatures on Venus, any water vapor there probably broke down into hydrogen and oxygen and escaped from the planet long ago.

Mars, on the other hand, is too cold and has too little atmosphere for liquid water to exist there now. Huge channel

Above: the windswept surface of Mars, photographed by Viking Lander 1, shows a dune field. Wind is probably the most active geologic process at the Martian surface today. Right: the Martian surface was carved into channels by ancient floods. The water clearly flowed around some existing craters, while others were formed by impacts after the water disappeared. This Viking 1 photo is about 120 miles (200 km) across.

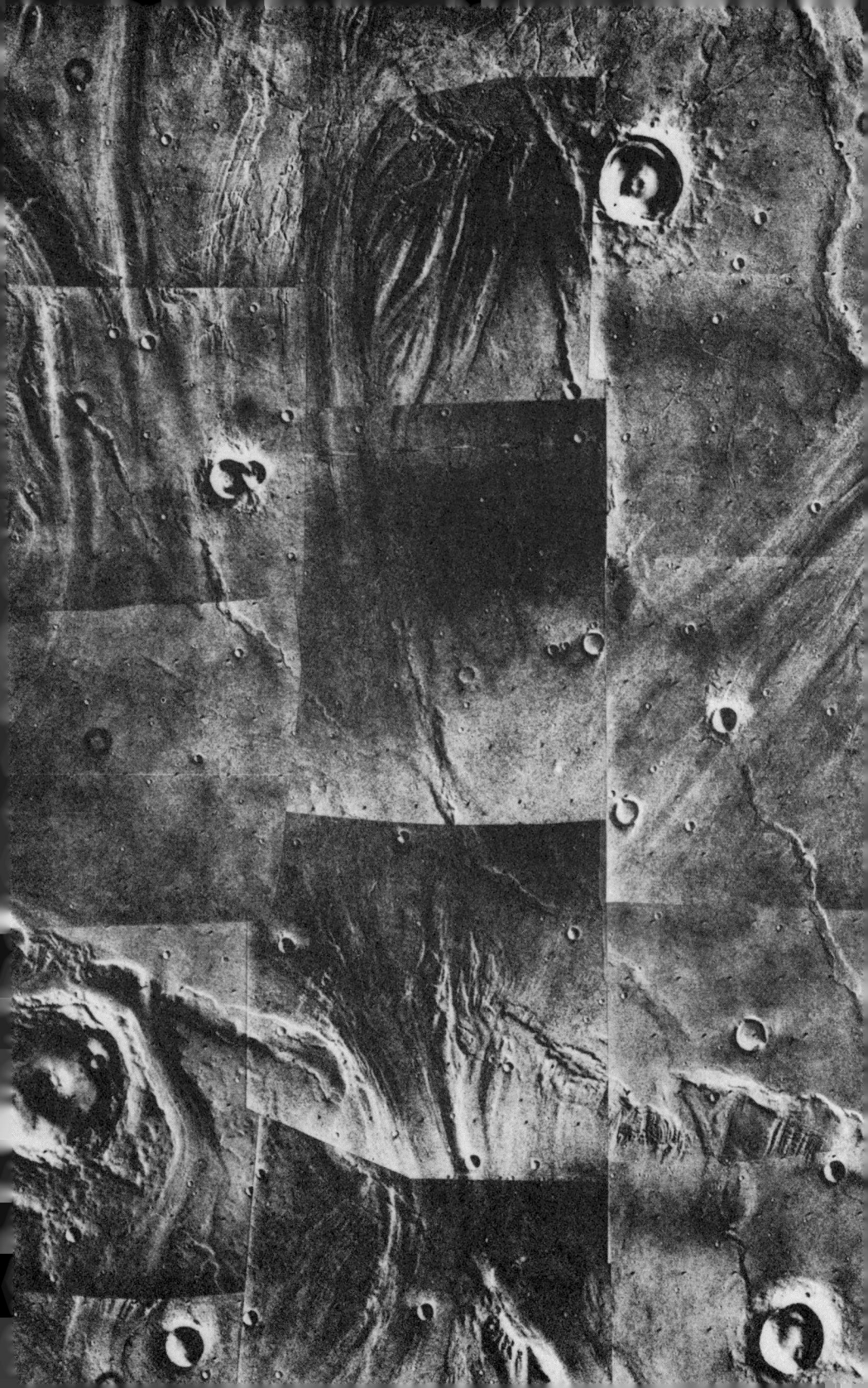

systems and layered rocks on Mars suggest that rivers may once have flowed across its surface in the past. Most of the floods probably happened several billion years ago. The Martian channels indicate that the climate must have been much warmer than it is now, and the atmosphere much denser. Understanding what caused a major climatic change on Mars would be a valuable step in understanding more about how climates change on Earth as well. The only traces of water at the surface now are in the morning frost and polar caps seen in the far north and south of the planet.

PEOPLE ON THE MOON

The closest planetary body to the Earth is our own Moon. It is so large, relative to the size of Earth, that the two are sometimes called a double planet system. Many photographs have been taken of the Moon, from Earth-based telescopes, the Ranger and Surveyor missions, and then from manned space missions. In 1969, the first person set foot on the Moon: NASA astronaut Neil Armstrong. With the return of rocks from the lunar surface to Earth, extraterrestrial geology was truly born.

Telescopic and photographic study gives some information about the age of lunar surfaces, but the dating methods only tell the ages *relative* to each other: which are older and which are younger. When the Moon rocks were brought back to Earth, scientists could calculate the age of the rocks in years, using radioactive elements in them.

From the Moon rocks returned by Apollo missions 11, 12, 14, 15, 16, and 17, planetary geologists found that the darker areas on the Moon are regions with basalt, the same dark igneous rock that makes up most of the ocean crust on Earth. These basaltic lavas flowed over the surface of the Moon until about 3.2 billion years ago. The lava flows created the darker, relatrively smooth areas on the lunar surface called **maria** (MAH-ree-ah). Since that time, no geologic activity besides cratering has occurred on the Moon.

The lighter-colored material on the surface of the Moon forms the lunar **highlands,** which are rougher areas above the basaltic plains. These highlands are composed of a rock called anorthosite, which is composed almost exclusively of one feldspar mineral. Anorthosite (ann-OR-tho-site) is found in only a few places on Earth, including the Adirondack Mountains of New York and some mountains in central Africa. The discovery of anorthosites on the Moon created considerable interest in the places where they occur on Earth.

Today, geologists are quick to point out that, even though discoveries on the Moon have already revolutionized our understanding of the Solar System, there is still much to be learned. A return flight to the Moon is likely before the end of this century.

One of the important questions that still remains is how and where the Moon was created. It may have formed in its current orbit around the Earth, or somewhere else in space. A recent theory suggests that the Moon was "splashed" from the Earth by a huge asteroid that hit the Earth before it had completely cooled. Because we do not even know how it formed, the Moon is a top candidate for a return visit.

Astronaut Harrison Schmitt is the only geologist to have walked on the surface of the Moon, during Apollo 17 in 1972. Another geologist is currently in NASA's Astronaut Program: Dr. Kathryn Sullivan, who made history by being the first American woman to walk in space in 1984. Perhaps a return to the Moon will see other geologists collecting rock samples on the maria and highlands.

TESTING THEORIES ON OTHER PLANETS

One of the major reasons for studying other planets is to learn more about the Earth. We have already learned a number of things about Earth history, including the importance of impact craters and the special conditions on Earth that permit life to exist. A major test of our understanding of Earth is still to come.

A basic question about plate tectonics is *why* it occurs on Earth. What size and composition are necessary before plate tectonics will happen on a planet? One way to find out is to see if other planets have plate tectonics. So far, plate movement has never been observed anywhere but on Earth.

Possible factors in controlling plate tectonics include the composition of the planet, its size, and its geologic history. The size of the planet may be particularly important; if this is true, then Venus, which is just slightly smaller than the Earth, would be most likely to have plate tectonics, too.

Because the surface of Venus is hidden by thick clouds of sulfuric acid and carbon dioxide, scientists have not yet been able to determine whether Venus has plate tectonics. This may change soon. The Venus Radar Mapper, now called Magellan, to be launched by NASA in 1988, will look through the clouds and provide information about the planet's surface. A series of successful landings by the Soviet Union's Venera program have already given scientists close looks at several regions on the surface of Venus.

Evidence that might show Venus has plate movement would include volcanic activity and earthquakes (Venus quakes). If Venus has these, it will be important support for our current understanding of plate tectonics on Earth. If Venus turns out to have no volcanoes or faulting, then we may need to consider our theories for what causes plate tectonics. This is just one example of the ways in which studying other planets increases our understanding of the Earth.

Geologist and astronaut Harrison Schmitt did field work in the Taurus-Littrow Valley on the lunar surface during the Apollo 17 mission in 1972.

CHAPTER 10
REVOLUTION AT THE EDGE OF THE SOLAR SYSTEM

Some say the world will end in fire,
Some say in ice.

—Robert Frost

You are standing on a planet covered by flowers of orange and yellow sulfur. Nearby volcanoes are erupting. Yellow ash is falling on you, and the sky is filled by the bright colors of Jupiter's atmosphere.

Does this sound like science fiction? A few years ago, geologists would have agreed. Recent discoveries, however, have shown that this is a good description of Jupiter's moon Io (EYE-oh). Exploration of space has caused a revolution in our understanding of the planets and moons at the very edge of the Solar System.

THE GAS GIANTS

All the outer planets of the Solar System except Pluto are very different from the smaller terrestrial planets. Jupiter, Saturn, Uranus, and Neptune are mostly huge clouds of gas that have low densities, large sizes, and cold temperatures. Somewhere far beneath their cloud tops, the overlying gas is so heavy that the hydrogen and helium become liquid or even solid because of the pressure. For this reason, the outer planets are sometimes called the "gas giants."

Of the outer planets, only Pluto might have a hard surface like that of the inner planets, but this distant planet is unusual in many ways. It seems to be a ball of rock and ice, but our views of it are small and dim because it is so far away. Astronomers noticed only in 1978 that Pluto had an unusual bulge on one side that might indicate it has a moon. Although the existence of this moon has not yet been proven, the satellite has already been given a name: Charon.

Because the outer planets don't really have hard, rocky surfaces, it is hard to discuss their geology. Some of their moons, however, are excellent subjects for extraterrestrial geology.

WORLDS OF ICE

Jupiter, Saturn, and Uranus have collections of moons that make them look like miniature solar systems. Some of the smaller moons may be asteroids that were captured by the strong gravity of the large planets. Most of the moons, however, seem to have a lot of water ice in them. These moons are called the "icy moons," and studies of their surfaces tell much about what ice is like at very low temperatures.

Some of the moons of these outer planets have surfaces that are extensively cratered and fractured, suggesting that the ice is so cold that it is really as hard as a rock. Other moons have very smooth surfaces, which may indicate the planet has been heated so much that the ice melted and erased any craters on the surface.

Dione, one of Saturn's heavily cratered moons, is about 700 miles (1120 km) across. Its composition is more than half water ice. The bright patterns may be a combination of debris scattered by impact cratering and ice deposits.

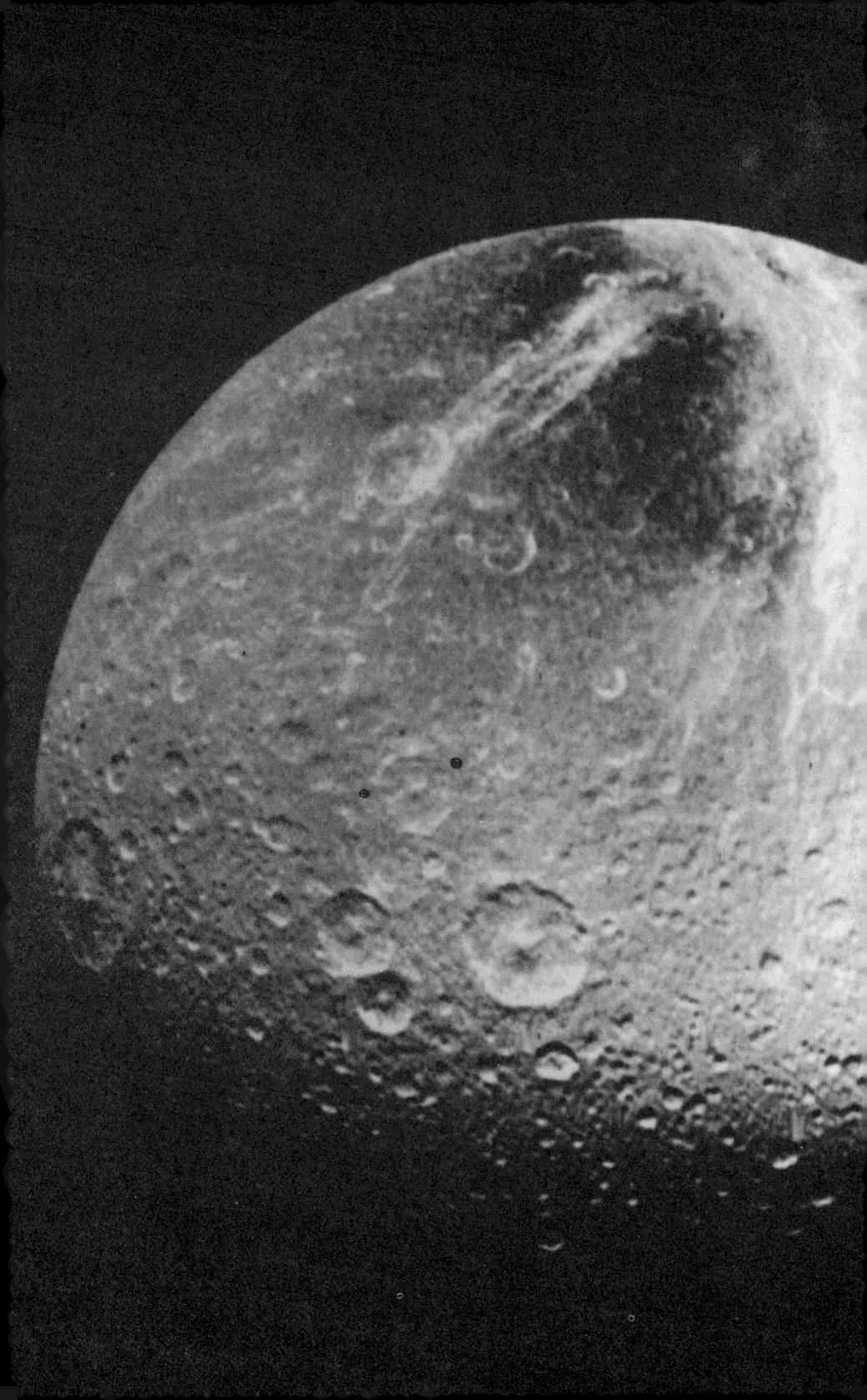

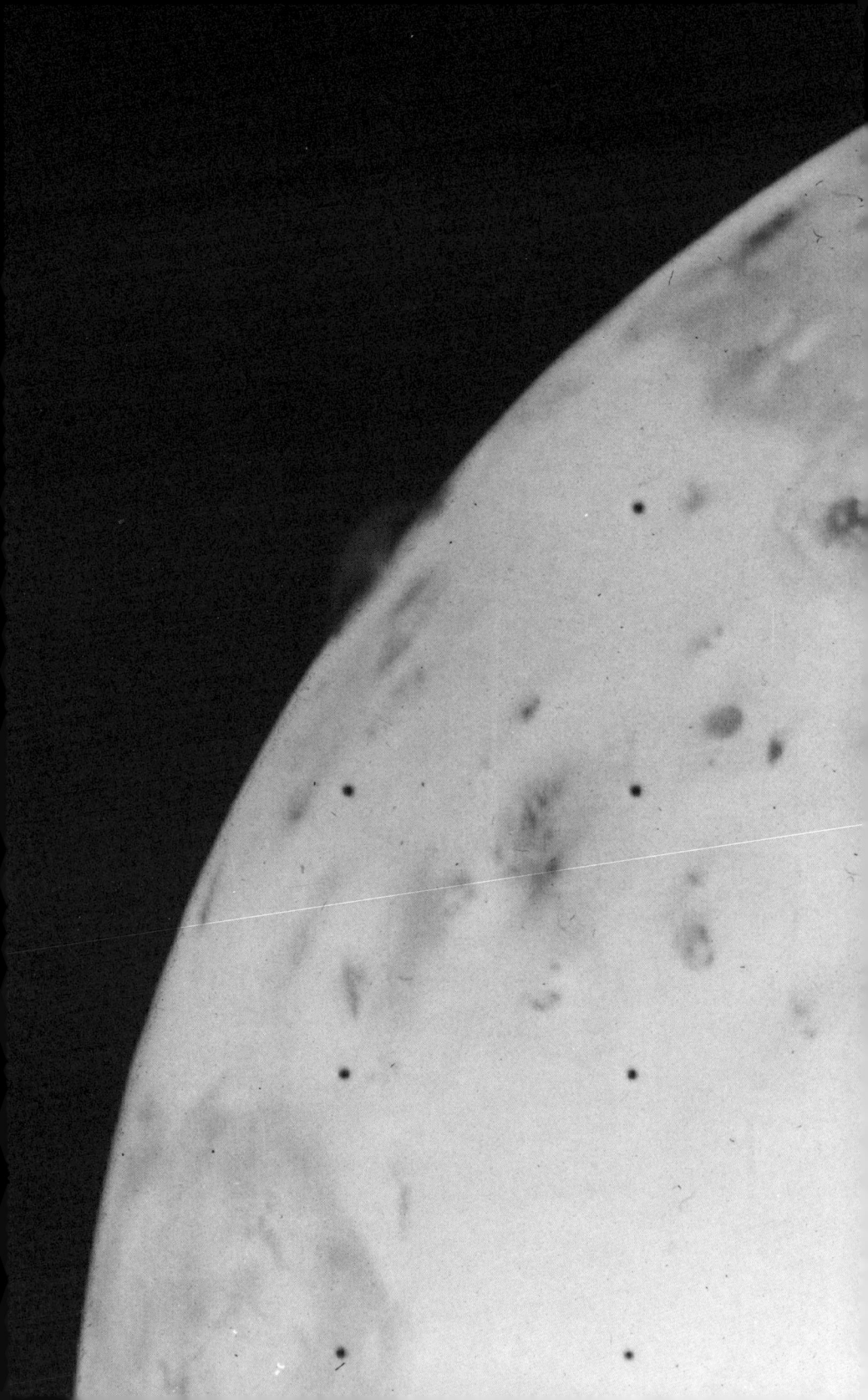

Many of the satellites of Jupiter, Saturn, and Uranus have been caught in only a few photographs from the Voyager spacecraft. The variety of surfaces is amazing. Some of the moons appear to be asteroids or comets trapped by the gravity of the large planets. Others have surface features with huge trenches, giant impact craters, and fine networks of fractures. One is half dark and half light in color. Others have more craters on one side than the other.

WORLDS OF FIRE

As the Voyager 1 spacecraft was passing Jupiter, one of the people who was looking at the photographs carefully was flight navigator Linda Morabito. In her office at the Jet Propulsion Laboratory in Pasadena, she studied a special set of photographs to be sure Voyager was on the correct course. The photographs were blurred and overexposed on purpose so that she could see the stars behind the planet and its moons.

In one of these photographs, she noticed a bright spot on one of Jupiter's moons. She first thought that something was wrong with the photograph, but further study showed that this moon really did have patches of light on its surface. What could this mean?

Morabito had discovered the volcanoes on Jupiter's moon Io. This is the only place in the Solar System besides Earth where active volcanoes have been observed erupting. The Voyager cameras also took pictures of some other eruptions on Io as they were happening. This is the same planetary body described at the beginning of this chapter.

The heat for the volcanoes on Earth and Io comes from very different sources. On Earth, radioactive elements deep

Jupiter's moon Io erupts liquid sulfur. This volcanic activity is very different from that on Earth, but Io is the only other place in the Solar System where volcanoes have been observed erupting.

within the Earth slowly break down, giving off heat. On Io, the heat source seems to be Jupiter. The gravity of Jupiter acts like a giant hand, squeezing the moon like a tennis ball as it orbits the larger planet. This heats up Io just as bouncing a rubber ball will heat it up by squeezing the air inside it. A bicycle tire will feel hot just after it has been pumped up for the same reason—the material (air) inside the tire heats up as it is pushed together.

When the Voyager spacecraft flew past Io, it photographed some spectacular plumes of sulfur as they were erupting on the moon. The surface of Io seems to be composed of flows of sulfur, which geologists are still trying to understand. Problems still to be solved include the chemistry of the sulfur and the relationship between its color and temperature. The surface of Io shows many shades of yellow, orange, and black, but the color patterns have not yet been interpreted completely.

A FROZEN EARTH?

One of the moons of Saturn also has a unique characteristic: Titan (TIE-tan) is the only moon we know that has an atmosphere. Until 1980, Titan was thought to be the largest moon in the Solar System because its atmosphere was so thick that scientists couldn't tell where the atmosphere ended and the surface began. When Voyager 1 flew by Titan in 1980, its careful measurements showed that the diameter of Titan was just a little less than that of Ganymede (GAN-ee-mead), Jupiter's largest moon. Therefore, Titan is the second largest moon in the Solar System.

Titan's atmosphere is composed of carbon dioxide and nitrogen, and the atmospheric pressure is about one and one-half times that on Earth. The amount of nitrogen in

Sunlight shines through Titan's thick atmosphere in this Voyager 2 photo of one of Saturn's moons. This view of the night side of Titan was taken from a distance of 560,000 miles (910,000 km).

Titan's atmosphere makes it quite similar in composition to Earth's atmosphere, but the temperatures are much colder than those on Earth. Titan has been nicknamed "The Earth in Deep Freeze," and it may be so cold that methane (a part of natural gas on Earth) may exist as a liquid. Titan may even have huge oceans of liquid nitrogen or methane that evaporate just like water on Earth, later falling as methane rain and snow.

Geologists and atmospheric scientists are interested in Titan because it has different conditions from all the terrestrial planets that have atmospheres. If Venus is an example of what could happen if Earth's temperature ever became too hot, then Titan shows us the Earth's fate if our planet cooled off.

RINGS AROUND THE PLANETS

In March 1977, astronomers knew that Uranus would pass in front of a bright star, and they were prepared to study the planet's atmosphere just as the star disappeared behind it. To their great surprise, they saw the star dim and brighten several times on both sides of Uranus. This evidence suggests that Uranus has several rings around it.

Unlike Saturn's bright, closely spaced rings, these seem to be dark and narrow, with wide gaps in between them. The Voyager 2 encounter with Uranus in January 1986 showed the rings are mostly composed of dust to boulder-sized material.

This was the first evidence that Saturn was *not* the only planet circled by rings of rock and dust. When Voyager 1 arrived at Jupiter, it photographed thin rings around that planet, too. Even Neptune is now believed to have a ring system. Only a few years ago, such rings seemed to be unique to Saturn. If Neptune's ring is real, then planetary rings are a common characteristic of the four largest outer planets. We must then ask why they have rings and the inner terrestrial planets do not. Could Earth and the other inner planets have faint, still undiscovered rings around them? If these are ever found, they will be a remarkable discovery.

A theory first proposed in 1985 suggests that Earth may have had a ring early in its history. This material might have been thrown into orbit by a major impact between a large planetary body and Earth, while the planets were still forming. The material would then have been gathered up within the orbit to form the Moon. If some of the terrestrial planets have had ring systems, then the inner and outer planets have more in common than geologists and astronomers ever imagined.

CHAPTER 11
GEOLOGY MEETS SPACE-AGE TECHNOLOGY

> *Once a photograph of the Earth, taken from outside, is available, once the sheer isolation of the Earth becomes plain, a new idea as powerful as any in history will be let loose.*
>
> —Fred Hoyle

Here on Earth, we have always looked out toward space, upward to the stars. Now, that view is changing. Space is rapidly becoming a place from which to look down and study Earth. Orbiting spacecraft are used to photograph and observe the largest features on the Earth's surface—mountain ranges, faults, and ocean basins. The experience of studying other planets has given scientists a new way to look at Earth. The use of space for research is possible only because of advances in technology within the past few years.

THE PLANETARY PERSPECTIVE

"The planetary perspective" involves seeing the Earth as a planet like any other—one planet among many bodies of varied size and composition, which, together with the Sun, form the Solar System. This view emphasizes the Earth's place within the Solar System.

Looking at Earth this way has already helped the study of other planets. Most of our information about other planets is based on photographs or other data collected by spacecraft. Only a few places on the surfaces of some of the inner planets have been seen in any detail. To compare Earth with the other terrestrial planets, photographs of Earth from the distance of space can be a great help.

Dr. James W. Head III, of Brown University in Rhode Island, has worked with space photography of the Moon, Mars, and Venus. In 1985, he commented on the importance of photos of Earth from space: "On the other planets, we often have a better understanding of global processes, such as wind activity on Mars, than we do of processes at a local and regional scale. On Earth, we know the local and regional processes, but we often don't understand what's happening at the global scale." Study of space photography of Earth is already changing that.

LANDSAT PHOTOS FROM SPACE

The Landsat Program, with a series of five orbiting spacecraft, began photographing Earth from space in 1972. By December 1984, more than 635,000 photos had been taken. Each of these images covers an area 115 miles by 115 miles (184 km), a total of 13,225 square miles (34,240 square kilometers). If the atmosphere was clear when the photo was taken, a land surface as small as about 260 feet across (80 m) might be identified. Landsat has already been used to study a variety of subjects, including large faults, patterns of

This Landsat photo shows the Salton Sea in southern California, just north of the U.S.-Mexican border; the Algodones dune field is to the lower right of the lake. The area shown here is about 180 miles (290 km) across.

land use, water resources, and oil and mineral deposits. The Landsat program was started by the U.S. government, but it has been taken over by private industry. This change has the support of many geoscientists who see the value of satellite photography in their work.

Photographs taken repeatedly over a long period of time can be especially valuable in studying changes at the Earth's surface. Geologic processes that show up in a series of large-scale photos include volcanism, fault movement, desert growth, climatic change, and coastal erosion. Large-scale images of Earth can also record changes in the types and health of plants growing on the surface, which also show changes in the climate. Satellite photographs can help scientists monitor the world's food supplies, and they may be used to warn of future shortages. In the coming years, these applications of space photography will be increasingly important.

VIEW FROM THE SPACE SHUTTLE

The most modern technologies for space photography involve radar and a Large Format Camera (LFC). Because radar depends on radio signals being reflected by distant objects, it can look through the thick clouds above the surface of Venus. If an exploratory mission is ever sent to Saturn's largest moon, Titan, radar will be needed to observe its surface through the thick atmosphere.

Radar cannot see far into water, but the surface conditions show up well. The first use of radar to study the Earth from space was in 1978. *Seasat* was an imaging system designed to study the ocean surface. It provided information on waves, major currents, and eddies in the Gulf Stream. One interesting discovery from *Seasat* was that wave patterns on the ocean surface are related to the topography of the sea floor.

Radar has also proved useful in studying features buried beneath the Earth's surface. The Shuttle Imaging Radar (SIR) has penetrated the cover of sand on the Saharan Desert to reveal a network of channels buried under the desert floor.

The SIR flown on the second flight of the space shuttle *Columbia* in 1981 was able to "see" 6 feet (2 m) or more beneath the sandy surface of the Sahara. The buried geologic features included river valleys, some of which were as wide as the Nile valley is today. This provides strong evidence for a wetter time in the recent geologic history of the area. Shuttle radar was also used on flight 41-G in October 1984. Radar from space promises to be useful in studying archaeology and water resources, as well as geology.

The Large Format Camera (LFC) was carried on the space shuttle for the first time in October 1984. It produces close-up images; objects that are just 33 feet (10 m) across on the ground can be identified in these photographs from space. This resolution is eight times better than in Landsat photographs. This new camera system also provides stereo coverage; two photographs of approximately the same area have enough overlap that, with special viewing equipment, an observer can look at the photographs and see the surface topography in three dimensions.

One example of the value of space photography comes from NASA's space shuttle mission STS-8 in September 1981. Geologists who have studied the pampas, the treeless grassland of central Argentina, had never understood the origin of a large deposit of volcanic ash and gypsum (a white mineral used in plaster and fertilizer). Then, a single photo taken by one of the astronauts in the space shuttle provided the answer: the image showed clouds of fine-grained dust being blown off the Andes Mountains and across the pampas to the east. Strong winds carry the ash and tiny gypsum crystals great distances and deposit them far away on the flat lands to the east. No observer on the ground could see a large enough area to realize that the source of the material was the Andes. An observer in Earth orbit could—and did—see this.

THE OCEAN FROM SPACE

Space photography is valuable for studying the oceans, as well as land surfaces. NASA's space shuttle mission in October 1984 had two earth scientists on board: Dr. Kathryn Sul-

Geologist and astronaut Dr. Kathryn Sullivan checks the Shuttle Imaging Radar antenna.

Space photography of the Strait of Gibraltar and the Mediterranean Sea is helping to answer questions about ocean currents.

livan, geologist and astronaut, and Dr. Paul Scully-Powers, an oceanographer. They both took many photos of the Earth, including 2,500 photographs of the oceans by Dr. Scully-Powers. These provide important information on ocean circulation.

One example of an area that has been studied from space is the Strait of Gibraltar. This narrow opening is between southern Spain and northern Africa, and it is the passageway between the Atlantic and the Mediterranean. The Strait has long been known to have dangerous currents. With the help of the space shuttle photographs, oceanographers at the Naval Ocean Research and Development Activity in Mississippi have constructed a theory for the deep circulation of ocean water through the Strait. This research will increase our understanding of ocean circulation, and will make the job of ship navigators (in the Mediterranean and elsewhere) a little easier.

MADE IN SPACE

The space shuttle itself also provides new opportunities for studying earth materials. Everything on Earth is affected by gravity, especially liquids, in which the molecules can move easily. In "zero-g," without the influence of gravity, mixtures of almost-uniform distributions of molecules can be created. When a solution cools, the crystals can be almost perfectly uniform, too.

The idea of manufacturing completely uniform crystals in space is an important part of the commercial use of space. Materials made in weightlessness are better mixed than those made on Earth. An alloy, a combination of two or more metals, is one example of this. Other valuable and useful materials that can be made in weightlessness include a variety of drugs.

On Earth, spheres tend to flatten slightly under the influence of gravity, but space manufacturing can create perfectly round balls of glass or other materials. The first commercial products to be "made in space" were tiny spheres of latex, a synthetic rubber, just 0.0004 inch (0.01 mm) in diameter. These spheres make precise measurements of microscopic objects possible. The first sale of these spheres in July 1985 marked the real beginning of space industry. Sales of very pure glass and alloys for use in electronics equipment have been predicted to reach $10 billion per year in the 1990s.

As the commercial uses of space expand, more of the costs will be handled by private industry. This means less of the expense will be carried by the federal budget and—ultimately—taxpayers. With luck, more federal money will then be spent on further study of Earth and the other planets.

GEOLOGY LABS IN WEIGHTLESSNESS

Almost all geologic processes are affected by gravity. Until geologists began studying other planets, they were usually only concerned with processes operating under Earth's gravity. The force of gravity is caused by the mass of an object, meaning the amount of matter it contains. The larger and more massive an object is, the greater its gravitational attraction will be. For Earth, the acceleration due to gravity, abbreviated **g,** is 32 feet per second per second (9.8 meters per second per second). For the Moon, it is only one-sixth that of Earth, so that on the lunar surface, anything would be only about 17 percent as heavy as on the Earth's surface. This is true whether the object is a grain of sand, a meteorite, or a person.

The differences in gravity on the various planets have an important influence on many geologic processes and events. A meteorite hitting Mercury or the Moon forms a different type of crater from one hitting the Earth.

Many of the features on the Martian surface are ten to 100 times larger than similar features on Earth. Although it is not the only explanation, the lower gravity on Mars may be a factor in why the landslides, canyon systems, and volcanoes on Mars are so large. The force of gravity that helps erode them is only 40 percent as strong as gravity on Earth.

The space shuttle or an orbiting space station offers a laboratory for studying the role of gravity. In zero-g, scientists can control the gravitational forces, creating conditions

that resemble those on planets smaller than Earth. Other processes that can be studied in the low-gravity environment of space include collisions between small particles (to study the processes when the planets first began to form out of gas and dust), the role of gravity in plate tectonics, the details of dust storms, and the processes associated with lava cooling and crystal settling.

In preparation for extended experiments on the shuttle or space station, earth scientists can rehearse their tests on NASA's KC-135 airplane. This plane can fly in long arcs; near the top of the curve, the plane's occupants experience up to 40 seconds of weightlessness. On a reduced scale, this is what your stomach feels when you go over the top of a rise on a roller coaster. Obviously it would be difficult to conduct full-scale experiments in this way, but the KC-135 is useful for making sure that an experiment will work. With the enormous cost of launching equipment into Earth orbit, pre-testing the experiments for a space laboratory is important.

REVOLUTIONS AND NEW TECHNOLOGY

The "planetary perspective" on Earth is possible only because of new technologies that allow the use of space for research. Experience in studying other planetary bodies from spacecraft helps point out new ways to study our own planet. The opportunities to observe geologic changes like faults and erosion make this valuable, as do the economic advantages of exploration for oil, gas, and mineral desposits. Studies from space will also give scientists more information about the processes of plate tectonics.

A new worldwide concern over global land use has been triggered by a variety of events, including recent famines in

The space shuttle Discovery was launched on its maiden voyage in 1984. The shuttle has many possible uses for geological experiments in weightlessness.

Africa. This has led to a number of national and international programs to study "global habitability"—the quality of life on Earth as it is controlled by environment. Important factors include water supplies, mineral resources, air quality, and soil productivity. These studies will rely heavily on space photography to record conditions and changes over large parts of the Earth's surface. With an understanding of the global environment, governments may be able to work together to prevent or reduce the damage of crop failures, desert expansion, and major floods.

Besides being a platform for studying Earth, space offers a laboratory for studying geologic processes under conditions that would be almost impossible to create at the Earth's surface. This includes both weightlessness and low-gravity conditions. Both of these allow scientists to produce pure materials for use in industry. The future will bring large-scale manufacturing in space of alloys, crystals, and drugs.

When the manned space program returns to the Moon or sends an expedition to Mars, geologists will find themselves exploring other planets again. The raw materials needed for space manufacturing and fuel systems may eventually be mined from other planetary bodies and processed in orbiting factories. When this happens, planetary exploration will cause another revolution in geology made possible by new technology.

GLOSSARY

Asteroid. A small, rocky body either left over from Solar System formation or created by the breakup of an older planet; most orbit the Sun between Mars and Jupiter, but some cross the Earth's orbit.

Asthenosphere. The layer of material inside the Earth, including the lower parts of the mantle; the material composing it is probably partially melted and able to flow.

Astronomical unit (A.U.). A unit for measuring large distances, equal to the average distance of the Earth from the Sun; equal to 93 million miles (150 million km).

Basalt. A dark, dense, fine-grained rock that cooled from a lava; rich in iron and magnesium and relatively poor in silica; most of the oceanic crust on Earth is basalt, as well as the low, dark lava plains on the Moon.

Comet. An accumulation of ice and dust; generally orbits the Sun at great distances, but only visible when orbit brings it close to the center of the Solar System.

Continental drift. The slow movement of the continents toward or away from each other as they are carried by plates moving across the Earth's surface; part of the theory of plate tectonics.

Fault. A fracture between two rock masses along which there has been movement; this movement usually causes earthquakes.

g. The acceleration due to gravity on Earth, equal to 32 feet per second per second (9.8 meters per second per second); gravitational attraction is related to the mass of an object.

Greenhouse effect. The trapping of radiation absorbed and then given off by the Earth's surface; the molecules that absorb the most energy are carbon dioxide and water; this warms the lower levels of the atmosphere.

Highlands. The higher, light-colored areas on the surface of the Moon.

Hot spot. A heat source in the Earth's mantle, which may cause hot magma to rise and spread outward at the Earth's surface; may be a factor in causing the movement of plates across the Earth's surface.

Hydrothermal. Related to hot water, often associated with heat sources near the edges of tectonic plates or hot spots.

Lithosphere. The rigid, outer part of the Earth, including the oceanic and continental crust and the upper part of the mantle.

Magma. Melted rock beneath the Earth's surface; when it reaches the surface, it is called lava; cools into an igneous rock.

Magnetometer. An instrument that measures the strength of a magnetic field; especially useful in studying the history of Earth's magnetism; magnetic reversals are recorded as alternating stripes of stronger and weaker magnetic intensity.

Manganese nodules. Layered, potato-shaped lumps on the deep ocean floor that contain up to 25 percent manganese and smaller amounts of nickel, iron, copper, and cobalt.

Maria. The dark, smooth areas on the surface of the Moon; relatively low in elevation and composed mostly of basalt.

Mass extinction. An episode in Earth history when a large number of organisms die, including all the members of some species; may be caused by drastic changes in the environment.

Paleomagnetism. The orientation of the Earth's magnetic field earlier in geologic time.

Plate tectonics. The processes associated with the slow movement of parts of the crust across the Earth's surface; the crust is divided into 12 large units and several smaller ones; most volcanic eruptions and earthquakes occur at the edge of these plates.

Polarity. The direction to the north and south magnetic poles compared to the geographic poles; "normal" polarity means the north arrow of a compass will point to the north geographic pole; during times of "reversed" polarity, the north arrow will point toward the South Pole of the Earth.

Radar. A process in which radio signals are sent toward an object and then reflected; the reflections are studied to determine the shape and other characteristics of the object; "radar" stands for **ra**dio **d**etection **a**nd **r**anging.

Radiometric dating. The use of naturally occurring radioactive elements to determine the age of rocks or other materials; depends on knowing the amount of radioactive material, how much of it has broken down, and the rate at which the process happens.

Rift zone. A place where crustal plates are separating and new crust is being created as rising magma cools.

Sea-floor spreading. The process that creates new crust at the mid-ocean ridges; associated with movement of crustal plates outward from the mid-ocean ridge.

Seismic activity. Earthquakes and related events; the study of seismic activity and the structure of the Earth's interior is called seismology.

Spreading center. The region where new crust is being formed as rising magma cools and hardens into igneous rocks.

Subduction. The process occurring in areas where crustal plates are coming together and one plate is pushed or pulled beneath another, which overrides it; volcanoes and earthquakes are often associated with these areas.

Submersible. A small, maneuverable research ship capable of taking one to five scientists deep below sea level to study the ocean floor directly.

Terrestrial planets. The four inner planets of the Solar System (Mercury, Venus, Earth, and Mars), plus the Earth's Moon; features they have in common include small diameters, rocky surfaces, and abundant heavy elements, making them dense.

FURTHER READING

Allen, Joseph P., with Russell Martin. *Entering Space: An Astronaut's Odyssey.* New York: Stewart, Tabori, and Chang. 1984.
Bolt, Bruce A. *Earthquakes: A Primer.* San Francisco: W. H. Freeman, 1978.
Briggs, Geoffrey, and Fredric Taylor. *The Cambridge Photographic Atlas of the Planets.* New York: Cambridge University Press, 1982.
Charig, Alan. *A New Look at the Dinosaurs.* New York: Facts on File, Inc., 1983.
Decker, Robert, and Barbara Decker. *Volcanoes.* New York: W. H. Freeman, 1981.
Duxbury, Alyn C., and Alison Duxbury. *An Introduction to the World's Oceans.* Reading, Mass.: Addison-Wesley, 1984.
Erlich, Paul, and Anne Erlich. *Extinction.* New York: Random House, 1981.
Francis, Peter. *Volcanoes.* New York: Penguin Books, 1976.
French, Bevan M. *The Moon Book.* New York: Penguin Books, 1974.
_____ and Stephen P. Maran, eds. *A Meeting with the Universe.* Washington, D.C.: NASA, U.S. Government Printing Office, 1981.

Gere, James M., and Haresh C. Shah. *Terra Non Firma: Understanding and Preparing for Earthquakes.* New York: W. H. Freeman, 1984.

Oakeshott, Gordon B. *Volcanoes and Earthquakes: Geologic Violence.* New York: McGraw-Hill, 1976.

O'Leary, Brian, and J. Kelly Beaty, eds. *The New Solar System.* 2nd ed. Cambridge, Mass.: Sky Publishing, 1982.

Short, Nicholas M., Paul D. Lowman, Jr., Stanley C. Freden, and William A. Finch, Jr. "Mission to Earth: Landsat Views the World." Washington, D.C.: NASA Special Publication 360, 1976.

Silver, Leon T., and Peter H. Schultz. "Geological Implications of Impacts of Large Asteroids and Comets on the Earth." Boulder, Colo.: Geological Society of America Special Paper 190, 1982.

Sullivan, Walter. *Continents in Motion.* New York: McGraw-Hill, 1974.

_____. *Landprints: On the Magnificent American Landscape.* New York: Time Books, 1984.

Turekian, Karl K. *Oceans.* 2nd ed. Englewood Cliffs, N.J.: Prentice-Hall, 1976.

Uyeda, Seiya. *The New View of the Earth.* New York: W. H. Freeman, 1978.

van Andel, Tjeerd. *Science at Sea: Tales of an Old Ocean.* New York: W. H. Freeman, 1981.

Wyllie, Peter J. *The Way the Earth Works.* New York: John Wiley and Sons, 1976.

INDEX

Italicized page numbers refer to illustrations.

Africa, 33, 113–114
Aleutian Trench, 36
Alvarez, Luis and Walter, 68–69, 70, 73
Alvarez theory, 73
Alvin, the, 41, *43*, 44
Animal behavioral changes, 64
Anorthosite, 89
Apollo missions, 81, 88, 89, *90*
Armstrong, Neil, 88
"Asteroid and the Dinosaur Theory," 72
Asteroids, 68–69, 72–73
Asthenosphere, 19, 36
Astronomical units, 72
Atmosphere, 85, 98–100

Bacon, Francis, 17

Basalt, 29, 88
Barringer (Meteor) Crater, 84
Black dwarf stars, 76–77
Boundary clay, 70

Caldera, 57
California Institute of Technology, 64
Cascade volcanoes, 54
Challenger Expedition, 36
Charon, 94
Columbia space shuttle, 107
Comets, 68–69, 72–73
Continental drift, 17, 19
Continents, 17, 27–33
Crandall, Dwight, 54
"Creep zones," 64
Cretaceous/Tertiary extinctions, 67–74

Darwin, Charles, 36
"Death Star," 76–77

—*121*

Deep sea drilling, 36–38
Dinosaur extinction, 67–74
"Do-it-yourself earthquakes," 66
Drake, Edwin, 47
Dust, cosmic, 78–79

Earth, 81–82, 84–85, 91
   creation of, 19
   gravity of, 111
   magnetism of, 27–28
   planetary perspective of, 113
   plate tectonics on, 84, 89
   possible rings around, 100–101
   study of from space, 103–104
Earth-like planets, 82, 84
"Earthquake engineering," 66
Earthquakes, 21–25, 61–66
East Pacific Rise, 41, *43*, 44
Electrical field changes, 57
Exclusive Economic Zone, 51
Extinctions, theories of, 75–80
Extraterrestrial geology, 81–91

Foraminifera, 70
French-American Mid-Ocean Undersea Study, 41

g, 111, 113
Ganymede, 98
Gaseous planets, 93–94

Geological clock, 76–77
Global land use, 113–114
Glomar *Challenger*, 38, *39*
Glomar *Pacific*, *39*
Glossopteris, 17
Gondwanaland, 21
Gould, Dr. Stephen Jay, 74
Gravity. See g
Greenhouse effect, 82
Gubbio, 68, 70

Halley's Comet, 73
Hawaiian-Emperor volcanoes, 32
Head, Dr. James W., 104
Heezen, Bruce, 25
Hess, Dr. Harry H., 25
Hot spots, 30–31, 36
Hubbert, M. King, 66
Hydrothermal vents, 41, 44

"Icy moons," 94, 97
Igneous activity, 84–85. See also Volcanoes
Impact craters, 69, 72, 84, *87*, *95*
Io, 93, *96*, 97–98
Iridium, 68–70

Jet Propulsion Laboratory, 97
Johnson Sea Link I, 44
Johnston, David, 58
"Joint Oceanographic Institutions Deep Earth Sampling," 38
Jupiter, 93–94, 97–98, 100

Krakatoa, 78
Kilauea volcano, *56*

—*122*

Landsat, 104, *105*, 106–107
Large-Format Camera, 106–107
La Soufriere volcano, 60
Laurasia, 21
Law of the Sea Treaty, 52
Lithospheric plates, 19, 21, 25
"Locked zones," 64–65
Lunar geology, 64–65, 88–89

"Made in space" products, 110–111
Magma, 22, 29–31, 54
Magnetic fields, 27–29
Mammoth Lakes, 54, 60
Manganese nodules, 48, *49*, 50
Manned space program, 114
Maria, 88
Mariana Trench, 36
Mars, 82, 84–85, *86*, *87*, 104, 111, 114
Mass extinction, 67–74
Matthews, D.H., 29
Mauna Loa volcano, 57
Mercury, 82, 84–85, 111
Mesozoic era, 33, 67
Mid-ocean ridges, 19, 38
"Moho," 37
Moon, *38*, 81, 88–89, 101, 104, 111, 114
Morabito, Linda, 97
Mount St. Helens, 54, *55*, 57–58, *59*, 79
Mullineaux, Donal, 54

NASA, 107, 110, 113

National Earthquake Prediction Evaluation Council, 66
Naval Ocean Research and Development Activity, 110
Nazca Plate, 30
Nemesis (star), 77
Neptune, 93
North American Plate, 22, 25
"Nuclear winter," 74

Ocean Drilling Program (ODP), 38
Oceans, 19, 25, 35–45, 47–52, 107
  and plate tectonics, 35–39
Olympus Mons volcano, 84
Oort cloud, 72–73, 77

Pacific Plate, 22, 25, 30
Paleomagnetism, 28
Paleontology, 70
Paleozoic era, 33
Pangaea, 21
Parkfield prediction, 65–66
Permian period, 17
Petroleum resources, 47–48
Photosynthesis, 69–70, 74
Pioneer spacecraft, 84
"Planetary perspective," 103–104
Plate tectonics, 15–25, 29–30, 33, 89
  and earthquakes, 61–62
  and ocean floor, 35–39
  and seismic gap theory, 65
Pluto, 77, 93–94

Polarity, 28
Precambrian era, 32
"Project Mohole," 37

Radar observation, 84–85, 106–107
Radioactive elements, 98
Radiometric dating, 29
Raff, Arthur, 28
Rangeley oil field, 66
Ranger missions, *83*, 88
Rift zones, 25, 29
"Ring of Fire," 21
Rings, planetary, 100–101
Rocky Mountain Arsenal, 66

San Andreas Fault, 22, 25, *63*, 64–65
Saturn, 93–94, *95*, 97–98, 100, 106
Schmitt, Harrison, 89
Scripps Institution for Oceanography, 28
Scully-Powers, Dr. Paul, 110
Sea-floor spreading, 25
Seasat imaging system, 106
Seismic gap theory, 64–65
Seismology, 53–60, 62
Shoemaker, Eugene, 73, 76
Shuttle Imaging Radar (SIR), 106–107, *108*
Sieh, Kerry, 64
Solar system movement, 93–101
  and mass extinctions, 78
Sounder research vessel, *40*
Soviet Union (U.S.S.R.), 51–52, 91

Space-age technology, 103–114
Space photography, 104, 106–107, *109*, 110
Space shuttles, 106–107, 110, *112*
Spreading centers, 25
  and ocean floor, 36
Strait of Gibraltar, 110
STS-8 mission, 107
Subduction, 22, 36
Submersibles, 25, 41, *42*, *43*, 44–45
  cost of, 45
Sullivan, Dr. Kathryn, 89, 107, *108*, 110
Surveyor missions, 88

Taurus-Littrow Valley, *90*
Tectonic plate collision, 21–22. *See also* Plate tectonics
Tenth planet (X), 77–78
Terrestrial planets, 82, 84
Tiltmeter, 54
Titan (moon of Saturn), 98, *99*, 100, 106
Tokarev, P.I., 57
Tolbachik Volcano, 57

United Nations, Law of the Seas Conferences, 51–52
United States Coast and Geodetic Survey, 28
United States Geological Survey (USGS), *40*, 54, 58, 60, 65–66, 73
United States Space Program, 37

University of California at
 Berkeley, 65
Upper mantle, 19
Uranus, 93–94, 97, 100
Uranium mining, 51

Venera program (U.S.S.R.),
 91
Venus, 82, 84, 104, 106
 and volcanic eruptions,
  84–85
 wind and water on, 85,
  91
Venus Radar Mapper (Magellan), 91
Viking Lander I, *86*, *87*
Vine, Fred, 29
Volcanic craters (calderas), 85

Volcanoes, 21–25
 cascading, 54
 eruptions, 53–60
 fire as source of, 97–98
 on other planets, 84–85
 over hot spots, 32
Voyager I expedition, 97–
 98, *99*, 100
Voyager 2 expedition, 100

Water level changes, 64
Wegener, Alfred, 17, 21
West Germany, 52
Wind, planetary, 85, 90
Woods Hole Oceanographic
 Institution, 41

"Zero-g," 110–111, 113

—125

ABOUT THE AUTHOR

Lisa A. Rossbacher is an associate professor of geology at California State Polytechnic University, Pomona. She was born in Virginia, attended college in Pennsylvania and New York, was a science reporter on National Public Radio in 1982, and received her Ph.D. in geology from Princeton University in 1983. Her current research is a study of water ice on the planet Mars, part of a larger NASA project to understand the geology and surface processes of the other planets in the Solar System. The search for features on Earth that resemble Martian landforms has taken her to Denmark, Sweden, and Finland. Dr. Rossbacher has published articles in popular and professional journals and written a book on careers in geology and the earth sciences. This is her first book for Franklin Watts.

SCIENCE IMPACTS

These books bring you up to date on what's new in science and technology. You'll be at the cutting edge with the scientists and engineers who are creating and testing theories, inventing products and machines, leading the way to the frontiers of space, to the conquest of disease, to the improvement of our environment.

TITLES IN PRINT:

THE GREENHOUSE EFFECT
by Kathlyn Gay

RECENT REVOLUTIONS IN ANTHROPOLOGY
by Maxine P. Fisher

RECENT REVOLUTIONS IN CHEMISTRY
by James A. Corrick

RECENT REVOLUTIONS IN GEOLOGY
by Lisa A. Rossbacher

RECENT REVOLUTIONS IN PHYSICS
by Albert Stwertka